# Unshakable Spirit

Stories of Compassion and Wisdom

# Unshakable Spirit

## Stories of Compassion and Wisdom

Kentetsu Takamori

**Translated by**
**Juliet Winters Carpenter**

**Ichimannendo Publishing, Inc.**
Los Angeles　Tokyo

*Unshakable Spirit: Stories of Compassion and Wisdom*
By Kentetsu Takamori
Published by Ichimannendo Publishing, Inc. (IPI)
970 West 190th Street, Suite 920, Torrance, California 90502
info@i-ipi.com    www.i-ipi.com
© 2012 by Kentetsu Takamori. All rights reserved.
Translated by Juliet Winters Carpenter.

NOTES TO THE READER:
In the process of producing the English translation, this book was adapted
by the author in close collaboration with the translator.
With the exception of the author's name, Japanese names are given in
traditional Japanese order, family name first, throughout the book.

Cover design by Endo Kazumi
Photographs by Yamamoto Tetsuji

First edition, December 2012
Printed in Japan
16 15 14 13 12    1 2 3 4 5 6 7 8 9 10

This book was originally published in Japanese by Ichimannendo Publishing
Co. Ltd. in two volumes under the titles of *Hikari ni mukatte hyaku no
hanataba* and *Hikari ni mukatte hyakunijusan no kokoro no tane*.
© 2000 and 2002 by Kentetsu Takamori

Distributed in the United States and Canada by AtlasBooks Distribution,
a division of BookMasters, Inc.
30 Amberwood Parkway, Ashland, Ohio 44805
1-800-BookLog    www.atlasbooks.com

Distributed in Japan by Ichimannendo Publishing Co. Ltd.
2-4-5F Kanda-Ogawamachi, Chiyoda-ku, Tokyo 101-0052
info@10000nen.com    www.10000nen.com

Library of Congress Control Number: 2012948942
ISBN 978-0-9790471-7-6

ISBN 978-4-925253-63-5

# INTRODUCTION

On March 11, 2011, an earthquake and tsunami of historic proportions struck off the northeast coast of Japan, wreaking extreme devastation. Official statistics list 18,716 dead or missing, with 393,353 homes destroyed.[*] The international community reached out quickly and with great warmth, not only to the areas directly affected, but to the nation as a whole. As a Japanese, I would like to take this opportunity to express my own profound gratitude.

International reports on the disaster were almost universally marked by admiration for both the selflessness of rescuers and the orderliness and gratitude with which refugees took up lives in crowded emergency shelters. A major Korean

---

[*] As of 22 August 2012

daily wrote of Japanese "endurance and neighborliness" in the face of adversity, while a Russian reporter marveled, "The locals keep their cool and do not panic." A *New York Times* columnist wrote admiringly about Japanese "selflessness, stoicism, and discipline," adding this comment: "The Japanese people have been magnificent, enduring impossible hardships with dignity and grace . . . I wish we might learn a bit from [them]."*

Why was there no chaos and looting in Japan? I think the French paper *Le Monde* was on target when it pointed out that Japanese learn from childhood the inevitability of change, which is a central tenet of Buddhism. Buddhist teachings on impermanence are deeply embedded in the Japanese soul, and this, wrote the paper, is what enables Japanese people to remain calm when disaster strikes.

Buddhism does indeed teach that everything in this world is transitory and in ceaseless flux. As expressed in the timeless words *shogyo mujo* (the impermanence of all things), change comes to one and all, whether gently or

---

* Nicholas Kristof, "The Japanese Could Teach Us a Thing or Two," *The New York Times*, 19 March 2011.

with sudden violence. Buddhism teaches us to quietly accept the feelings of sadness and grief that naturally arise when we come face-to-face with this truth and, at the same time, shows how to transmute those feelings into positive, forward-looking energy.

Harmony, effort, and patience are three traits that have become representative of our nation, and all three have their roots in Buddhism. Prince Shotoku (574–622), Japan's first great patron of Buddhism, wrote a Seventeen-Article Constitution that begins with this exhortation, familiar to all Japanese down the centuries: "Cherish harmony." But as Buddhism makes clear, human nature is desperately selfish. Setting aside self-interest to band with others is never easy. Harmony cannot exist without effort, and sustained harmony requires the cooperation and effort of all. The spirit that values efforts to promote harmony rises naturally from Buddhism.

Like harmony and effort, the patient acceptance of adversity—as seen in the recent disasters—is another Buddhist ideal. Ask any Japanese person how they can be so patient and you will likely be told *shikata ga nai*, "it can't be helped." The idiom expresses resignation, but not despair. The original form of the Japanese verb for "to be resigned" (*akirameru*) means literally "to see clearly" (*akiraka ni miru*). When we see clearly the three elements of the law of cause and effect—the law that forms the core of Buddhism—we can accept uncomplainingly all that befalls us.

Good actions yield good results (happiness).

Bad actions yield bad results (unhappiness, disaster).

The seeds each person sows yield outcomes that, for good or for ill, determine that person's fate.

Making efforts to do good is bound to yield good results. Knowing this leads people to avoid doing wrong even when no one is looking. The reason so many Japanese people affected by the disaster responded with neighborly sympathy, helping one another instead of resorting to violence and looting, is surely because deep down they understand that positive actions lead to happiness.

Life, as Śākyamuni Buddha taught long ago, is suffering. The slings and arrows of life come at us continually.

Look straight at the cause of your sorrows, examine yourself, and aim higher. In this way you can get up again however many times you are knocked down. The Buddhist way of life, based on this kind of clarity of vision, is full of strength and resilience.

Our nation will emerge from this calamity with vigor, just as it did nearly seventy years ago, when Japan rose from the ashes of war with indomitable spirit.

In the meantime, the remarkable outpouring of goodwill from around the world has been a tremendous encouragement. How can we best respond? Only by sharing Buddhism, the philosophy underlying the unshakable spirit of the Japanese people. That strong desire lies behind my decision to share these essays with the English-speaking world.

The stories and anecdotes in this book are not all related to Buddhism. They are full of variety, ranging from historical incidents to family problems. Yet each one has something to teach about Buddhist truth, which permeates time and space. I earnestly hope that this little book may enable people the world over to share in the precious teachings of Buddhism and acquire an unshakable spirit.

October, 2012

Kentetsu Takamori

# Contents

# 1

## When Disasters Strike
## in Quick Succession

A single swordsman fending off dozens of attackers at once: such scenes, a staple of Japanese television shows and storytelling, are pure fiction. Chiba Shusaku, once the most famous swordsman in all Japan, used to say, "If I were surrounded by three swordfighters with some understanding of swordsmanship, I could never win." Asked what he would do if he faced three or more attackers, he replied, "Make a run for it." He would run for dear life, and only when a certain distance had opened between himself and his enemies would he turn and cross swords with whoever was first in line. When that one succumbed, he would take to his heels again before turning to dispatch the next. As he went on in this fashion, those bringing up the rear would eventually flee, he said.

In life, disasters can and do strike in quick succession.

Victims of natural calamities like earthquakes, typhoons, volcanic eruptions, and floods lose everything they have built up, and are devastated. Illness, traffic accidents, forced separation, the loss of a loved one, anxiety over impending old age, worries over children, breakdowns in relationships—such troubles rob us of a sense of purpose and leave us sinking in an ocean of sadness. Why am I so sickly? Why does disaster stalk me? Why can't I rise in the world? One comes to feel like a magnet for calamity. The urge arises to end it all and escape.

The story is told of a foolish man who became thirsty and went in search of water. He came to a river of abundant fresh water, but made no move to drink a drop. When asked why not, he replied, "I'd give anything to drink my fill, but there's just too much water here. I could never drink it all. I don't know what to do." His listeners burst into laughter.

Even if we cannot drink the river dry, we can drink enough to slake our thirst. When difficulties and disasters strike all at once, we need to deal with each one separately, doing what we can with full sincerity, reflecting that everything that happens to us is the result of seeds we ourselves have planted. Then we are likely to make an unexpected breakthrough.

# 2

## The Bride Who Wept with Gratitude
## Toward Her Mother

The day after her wedding, a young bride knelt before her new mother-in-law and asked, "What shall I do today?"

The older woman said kindly, "My dear, there's no hurry. You must be worn out, so just rest."

"I'm not a bit tired. I'm not a terribly good seamstress, but if you like, I could help with the sewing."

"Why, that's very thoughtful of you. Perhaps I will ask you to sew me a kimono, then. Take all the time you want."

The older woman produced some crimson crepe fabric. Anxious to please, the bride stayed up late to finish the task. In the morning she greeted her mother-in-law and said, "I finished the crepe kimono. I'm afraid the workmanship is clumsy, but please have a look."

The older woman was surprised at how quickly the kimono had been made, and doubly surprised when she saw the beautiful needlework. She was so pleased with the garment that she couldn't help taking it to show the neighbors.

Happiness welled up in the bride, but at the same time she wept to think of her own mother, who used to scold her day after day: "What kind of stitches are these! I never saw such a clumsy child. You've got to apply yourself!" Forced to rip out her stitches over and over again, she had been angry and resentful at the time. Yet now, thanks to her mother's scolding and strict training, her work had won high praise.

The young woman was struck for the first time by the thoughtfulness that lay behind her mother's actions, and she shed tears of gratitude.

> It is not hate
> that moves the hand
> striking snow from bamboo.

Bamboo that is heavily laden with snow often bends

and breaks. Striking the branch to clear away the snow allows the bamboo to thrive.

# 3

# "Win Big Today, Lose Big Tomorrow"

*Trust Is a Huge Asset*

Sengai, the chief priest of a Zen temple in Kyushu two centuries ago, left a large number of ink paintings. Among them was a painting of an account book and an abacus, with this accompanying poem:

> Raise your hand and they go away,
> lower your hand and they come to you.
> Forget it not, forget it not!

On an abacus, when you lift your hand the beads rattle away from you, and when you lower your hand they rattle toward you. In the same way, if you skimp on quality and raise prices, customers will drift away, but if you increase quality and lower prices, customers will flock to you and your business will thrive. The poem warns merchants not to forget this basic principle.

There's an old saying, "Folding screens and businesses collapse unless they are a little crooked." In other words, just as a folding screen must be bent if it is to stand up, so businesspeople have to bend the rules if they want to succeed. Some people make this claim to justify shady practices, but they are wrong. Another saying goes, "Win big today, lose big tomorrow." In other words, if you run a crooked business you may come out ahead in the short term, but you are sure to lose trust and find your way blocked in the end.

Trust is a huge asset. The Chinese character for "making money" combines elements meaning "trust" and "person": the trusted person succeeds.

# 4

## Solidarity Can Be More Important than Numbers

Greater numbers often bring victory on the battlefield, but there is another, even more essential factor: solidarity. The battle of Sekigahara in the year 1600, a fight for ultimate power after the death of warlord Toyotomi Hideyoshi, eloquently illustrates that truth.

Tokugawa Ieyasu's army of the east faced off against Ishida Mitsunari's army of the west, but they were clearly outnumbered. The armies' troop strength was so mismatched that three centuries later, a German staff officer assigned to advise the Japanese Imperial Army looked at a map of battlefield positions at Sekigahara and marveled, "It's unbelievable that the army of the west could have lost!"

Sekigahara was the largest battle the world had ever seen, with twenty-five thousand muskets in all. In firepower as well as manpower, the west had the clear advantage. Then why did they lose? Because they could not match the army of the east in solidarity, that essential ingredient of victory.

Ishida Mitsunari, Hideyoshi's retainer and heir, was not a popular figure; Kato Kiyomasa, Fukushima Masanori, and other courageous generals trained by Hideyoshi rose up against him. Moreover, discord between Hideyoshi's widow and Lady Yodo, his concubine, led to the treachery of Kobayakawa Hideaki at Sekigahara. Under those conditions, for the army of the west the battle was as good as lost from the start.

The western army at Sekigahara lacked solidarity, the key to victory.

# 5

## Why Children Don't Answer
### *Teaching by Example*

A Japanese college professor once told this personal story.

"I have a five-year-old son. Until a few months ago, whenever anyone called his name he would answer '*Hai!*' ['Yes'] in a loud voice. But then for some reason he stopped doing it. I gave it some thought and realized I was to blame. I'd been so swamped with work that often when my wife called me I wouldn't answer, but just go on working in silence. My son must have seen me doing that and quit answering when spoken to. I tried various things to get him to respond, but nothing worked.

"Then it hit me. The most important thing is for me myself to answer clearly when I'm called.

"And what do you know! Soon enough he began saying

'*hai*' enthusiastically when we called his name. The atmosphere in our house really changed for the better."

Many men who graduated from college years ago spend the rest of their lives toiling at their jobs, hard-pressed and joyless. Why then, as fathers, do they rant about the need to do well in school? "Study hard and get into a good college," they say. "That's all your mother and I ask. Do it for us! Study! Study! Study!"

It makes no sense to children.

"Why should I study hard to get into college and then study even harder to graduate, just so I can end up like my old man?" they wonder. "He does nothing but work all the time. I can't work any harder than him. Maybe I don't have what it takes to keep on living."

Too often, a child looks at his parents and loses hope. Trembling with worries and anxiety, he may suffer a nervous breakdown or even take his own life.

True education is education by example.

# 6

## "I Lost My Heart to Her Smile"

A newly married couple moved into the house next door. "Young people today are so wrapped up in themselves," commented the neighbor to her husband. "The wife probably won't be very neighborly."

A week later, she went outside with her baby just as the new neighbor was getting home. "Cold out, isn't it?" said the new neighbor, and then added with a smile, "Oh, what a beautiful baby! The little dear! The way she laughs is just adorable."

That night the neighbor said to her husband, beaming, "You know something? You just can't tell about people. That young wife who moved in next door, for example— she turned out to be a lovely person, just as charming as she can be!"

This is a true story about a young woman working as a waitress in a department store café who married into a wealthy family. The mother of the groom was impressed by the young woman the first time she saw her.

"When I ordered a light meal at that café, the waitress who brought it said, 'Sorry to keep you waiting' and set the food in front of me. Then with a smile and a nod she said, 'Enjoy your meal!' There was nothing false about her smile. It was sweet and genuine.

"Most servers apologize for keeping you waiting, slam down the food, and then disappear. But she set down the tray, gently adjusted it in front of me, and said 'Enjoy.' I was won over by her words and her smile."

Gentle words and consideration can shape a person's future.

# 7

## The Essence of Beauty

Long ago in India there was a rich man whose daughter was regarded as a paragon of beauty, and indeed, she was lovely to look at. Her father was enormously proud of her. He would take her with him wherever he went and say rash things like, "A thousand pieces of gold to anyone who says my daughter isn't beautiful!" Indeed, the girl's face and figure were so lovely that all who saw her, men and women alike, were captivated.

One day the father came up with a scandalous notion. Since everyone was so charmed by the sight of his daughter, he decided to show her to noble Śākyamuni, and force even him to acknowledge her beauty. With the girl in tow, he set out.

After seeing the girl, Śākyamuni said quietly, "I do not

find her beautiful in the least. Yes, her appearance is attractive, but what is far more important than outward appearance is the beauty of the heart. Inner beauty is true beauty."

Every woman dreams of becoming beautiful. True beauty, however, lies not in the face or figure, but in the heart, as Śākyamuni said. A pure heart as clear as the autumn sky is the essence of beauty, and it is this heart that men as well as women need to cultivate.

The rich man was chastened by Śākyamuni's words.

# 8

# Feeling Puffed Up with Vanity
# Leads to Hell

The following story is taken from the literary classic *Essays in Idleness* by the medieval Japanese priest and scholar Kenko.

A legendary saint by the name of Kume sailed freely through the skies, riding on a cloud. There were no airplanes in those days, so it must have been a thrilling experience indeed. One afternoon, he looked down complacently on the world below, where a river ran quietly through the broad Yamato plain.

Squatting on the riverbank was a lovely young woman, humming as she did her washing. With no one else around, she had pulled her skirt up comfortably, and her knees were spread apart.

Though Kume was a man of great spiritual discipline, the sight of those bare legs was too much for him. Forbidden lustful thoughts rose one after another in his mind.

Just then, he lost his magical powers and plummeted to earth, never to fly again. He founded a temple on the spot and devoted the rest of his life to asceticism.

Of course no one, not even a sage, can possibly ride through the sky on a cloud. This is a metaphor for self-conceit, for the attitude that looks down from a great height and boasts, "I am an enlightened sage!"

Nothing is so dangerous as conceit, which causes us to look down on others for any of a hundred reasons: I'm rich, I have a Ph.D., I'm the company president, I'm gorgeous . . .

Until Japan was defeated in World War II, the nation was full of conceit. Puffed up with the conviction that they were a divine race, the Japanese annexed other countries and ruled them. The result was the ruin of the country, an infamous descent into hell. People can climb a mountain peak, but they can't stay there long. Let no one forget that being carried away with your own self-importance is the beginning of hell.

# 9

## Anger Is the Enemy

A certain Swiss philosopher was famous for his even temper. A woman who worked as his housekeeper for ten years swore that she never saw him so much as frown in anger.

One time a prankster offered to pay her if she could make her employer, a friend of his, lose his temper. The housekeeper thought and thought, and decided what to do. Her master liked his bed neatly made, so she deliberately left it unmade. The next morning she fully expected a reprimand, but he only commented, smiling, "Say, last night when I went upstairs, the bed wasn't made."

One night wasn't enough, she thought. The next night she left the bed unmade again. In the morning he said, "You know, the bed wasn't made last night either. You must have been busy. Make it tonight, will you?" But she didn't.

On the third morning the philosopher summoned her to his study and said, "I see you didn't make the bed again. You must have your reasons for not doing it. Anyway, I've gotten used to making it myself, so from now on I'll take care of it."

The housekeeper had expected a thorough dressing-down. At this show of generosity, she broke down, fell at her employer's knees, and sobbed out the whole story, begging his forgiveness. The philosopher never left off smiling. He bore this undeserved ill treatment with admirable patience.


Unchecked anger is a raging flame that devours all goodness. The following story illustrates the danger.

Once, due to a servant's carelessness, a rich man's dinner was eaten by a lamb. The servant received an angry rebuke, and for spite he threw hot coals onto the offending animal. The lamb's fleece caught fire, and the animal ran in panic into the barn.

The fire spread to thousands of head of sheep, and in the end the rich man's barn and home burned to the ground.

One person's anger spreads out in waves without end. Know that anger is the enemy, and patience is the foundation of long-lasting peace.

He who expresses anger with his mouth is an inferior man.

He who grits his teeth and does not express his anger is a middling man.

He who shows no sign of anger even when he is boiling with rage is a superior man.

# 10

## Integrity Above All

Kumazawa Banzan, a seventeenth-century Confucian scholar, looked everywhere for a teacher. One night he heard an inspiring story from a merchant he shared lodgings with. This was the merchant's tale:

"One time when I was visiting Kyoto, I lost two hundred gold coins that belonged to the man I worked for. I went into despair and resolved to make amends by taking my life. Late that night, someone knocked at my door and insisted on seeing me. I opened the door to find the groom of the horse I had ridden that day.

"'After I left you here I went home,' he said, 'and when I checked the horse's saddle I found all this money. It can only be yours. I knew you would be upset, so I rushed over to return it to you. Now I can finally relax.'

"And with those words, he held out the missing money. I was saved—and overwhelmed that there should be a man so upright in this day and age. Uneducated he might be, but he had the heart of a saint. I offered him sixteen gold coins as a token of my appreciation, but he shook his head.

"'I haven't done anything great or notable,' he said. 'All I did was bring you back what was yours to begin with. I don't deserve a reward for doing anything so unremarkable.'

"I was so moved by the man's purity of heart that I questioned him further. He told me, 'Where I come from, there is a great man named Nakae Toju. He says that no matter how poor a man may be, he should never pester others for more money, or accept ill-gotten gains, or chase after personal gain. He says that a man should protect his integrity above all. My coming here tonight is simply a reflection of his teachings, and nothing special in the least.'

"And so," concluded the merchant, "the groom's behavior showed the influence of a man named Nakae. What a splendid teacher he must be!"

This account convinced Kumazawa that there could be

no teacher for him but Nakae Toju, the Confucian philosopher known as "the saint of Omi."

# 11

## "Your Fly Is Open, Too"

*Observe the Behavior of Others and Correct Your Own*

Back in the early postwar era in Japan, when cars were scarce, everyone got around by bus or train. One day I found myself riding on a nearly empty bus. I picked a seat, sat back, and relaxed. Across from me sat a distinguished-looking man in his fifties whose fly, I couldn't help noticing, was unbuttoned. (This was in the days before zippers came into common use.) I contemplated what to do, but of course he had to be told. I slipped over beside him and quietly let him know the situation, man-to-man. Some men might have taken offense at being told such a thing, but not he. After a momentary look of surprise, he thanked me politely and gave a rueful smile as he covered himself with the magazine he'd been reading and did up his fly.

Relieved, I returned to my seat, planted my feet on the floor, folded my arms, and looked around again. Lo and behold, the distinguished-looking man across the way got up and came over to sit beside me. Wondering what on earth he could want, I tensed with expectation as he brought his lips to my ear and murmured with a smile, "Your buttons are undone, too."

With a start, I reached down and realized he was right. My cheeks burned in embarrassment. To cover my confusion, I gave a rueful smile and thanked him.

The proverb has it, "Observe the behavior of others and correct your own."

I was made to realize then that even such apparently obvious sayings must never be taken lightly.

# 12

## Śākyamuni Took the Most
## Painful Path of All

This incident occurred while Śākyamuni Buddha was still an ascetic. A wounded dove came flying up to him and said desperately, "I'm being attacked by an eagle. Please save me!" Śākyamuni gently tended to the trembling dove and hid it in his bosom.

Before long, a famished eagle came by and asked, "Didn't a dove fly this way?"

"It is here in my bosom," Śākyamuni told him.

"Now I can live longer," said the eagle in relief. "Please give me the dove. It's the one I found when I was about to starve. Without it, I will certainly die."

To keep the eagle alive, the dove would have to die, and if the dove were saved, the eagle would have to perish. Trapped, Śākyamuni made an incredible decision.

"My dear eagle," he said, "does it need to be a dove to save you from starvation?"

"Not at all," said the eagle. "As long as I eat something with the same  amount of flesh as the dove, I can recover."

"Then, how about this? I will offer you an equivalent amount of my flesh, so will you let the dove go?"

Having obtained the eagle's consent, Śākyamuni sliced off flesh from one of his thighs and compared it with the dove's weight, but it was far from enough. He then sliced off flesh from his other thigh, but it was still not enough. He sliced off pieces of his body here and there and offered his own flesh to the eagle.

The eagle, his belly now full, was happy and content. The dove, who had come so close to dying, was also happy. Seeing their two lives saved, Śākyamuni too rejoiced.

To teach an eagle the heart of compassion is virtuous. To teach a dove about the universal law of cause and effect may also be necessary at times. But Śākyamuni took the most difficult and painful path of all, because that path is supreme and unsurpassed.

# 13

## "Pray That I Will Never Die"

Having heard of the great virtue of the hermit monk Ryokan, an eighty-year-old man came to him with a request. "There are things I still want to do, so I'd like you to pray that I live a little longer."

"About how long do you want to live?" inquired the monk. "Unless I know the age you have in mind, I can't say the prayer."

"Well, ninety would give me only ten more years, so I'll say an even hundred."

"Another twenty years. Very well, but when you turn a hundred and one, you'll have to die. All right?"

"Can I ask for a little more time?"

"How much more? Tell me."

"How about till I'm a hundred and fifty?"

"A hundred and fifty? Is that enough?"

"I don't want to ask too much . . ."

"Don't hold back."

Little by little the old man's request spiraled up. He wanted to live to be two hundred—no, three hundred—no, five hundred years old! Amused, Ryokan couldn't contain himself. "As long as you're asking, you might as well go all the way. Go on, tell me what it is you want," he urged. The man finally said what was really on his mind.

"All right then. I'd like you to pray that I will never die."


A man threw a party for his friends and served blowfish, a prestigious culinary treat but one that can be deadly. Everyone was too afraid of the possibility of being poisoned to try it. Then along came a traveler. They offered him a plateful, and when he came to no harm, they all helped themselves in relief. Afterwards someone asked the traveler if he had enjoyed the dish.

"You all ate yours already?" he answered. "In that case I'll eat mine."

Sengai, a revered Zen priest, lay on his deathbed. His followers handed him a paper and brush and asked him for some final words of wisdom. He wrote simply, "I don't want to die."

The followers had been eagerly looking forward to some profound last words. Seeing what he had written, they felt consternation, afraid that his reputation would suffer irreparable damage. After conferring, they came up with a plan. "What you wrote is fine, but if you could add a little something to it . . ."

Sengai consented, but when he handed the paper back and they read it they were flabbergasted. He had added two words: "I really, really don't want to die."

Everyone's ultimate wish, it seems, is the same.

# 14

# "I Do Not Wish to Be
# a Slave to Riches"

A young man once worked for a wealthy merchant. He was extremely bright and talented, and the merchant thought highly of him. One day the merchant summoned the lad and said, "You have a knack for business. Here are one hundred gold coins. I want you to use them as capital for whatever business you like, and return them to me tenfold."

Overjoyed, the youth set out to do as he'd been told. Instead of starting a big venture that might only fail, he decided to build up a small business and earn a slow but steady profit. He bought paper scraps, made them into tissues, and sold them for a small amount. In three years he had earned three hundred gold coins, and in five years, a thousand.

He went back to his employer and reported, "I increased the gold you gave me tenfold. Here it is."

His boss was impressed. "I knew you had talent, but this is amazing! Now go out and do the same thing again."

Several years later, the younger man returned with ten thousand gold coins, as promised. His boss praised him again and instructed him to increase his capital tenfold once more, which he did in only three years' time. Still unsatisfied, the master told him to come back with a million gold coins.

This time the younger man drew himself up and replied, "Turning one hundred thousand gold coins into a million is far easier than turning a hundred into ten thousand. But however much money one has, it is never enough. Human desire knows no bounds. I do not wish to be a slave to limitless desire. Gold serves no purpose when we are dead."

And so he firmly rejected his master's wishes and became a Buddhist monk.

One day a man paid a call on an older man who lived alone and was gravely ill. "You are really sick, my friend," he said. "Why don't you go into the hospital?"

"I can't afford it," came the answer.

"You own land, don't you? Why not sell some of it and use the proceeds to pay for your treatment?"

His friend's eyes opened wide in astonishment. "Heavens no! Why would I do a thing like that?"

"Well, because you're sick."

"Yes, but you never know what may happen down the road. I'm saving that land for an emergency."

"This *is* an emergency!" insisted the old man, but to no avail.

One week later he received word of his friend's passing.

> I peer
> Into the depths of the abyss
> Where I must fall—
> Ah, how unfathomable,
> the pit of my desires.

# 15

# The Quick-witted Page and
# the Hot Coal

On New Year's Day at Edo Castle, the shogun Tokugawa Yoshimune was about to receive ceremonial congratulations from various lords, and went with several pages to see that all was in readiness. He walked into the room just as an official was placing hot coals in the brazier with a long-handled tool. Flustered at the shogun's sudden appearance, the official dropped a live coal on the tatami matting. He cried out in shock, but it was too late. The matting had started to smolder and smoke.

Just then one of the pages behind the shogun, a boy of twelve or thirteen, darted out, grabbed the coal in his long kimono sleeve, and tossed it out into the garden. Then he dipped his burning sleeve in the cistern on the veranda.

Everyone let out a sigh of relief at the boy's quick-witted action. The shogun looked him over carefully and then said, "Stand up and stretch out your arm." The boy did so. "Turn it over."

"Yes, sire."

"That's strange. You doused the fire in your sleeve with water just now, didn't you?"

"Yes, sire."

"And yet your sleeve isn't either scorched or wet!"

"Yes, it is. See?" The boy revealed the blackened, wet sleeve of his under-kimono. Damaging his holiday kimono would have meant he couldn't perform his role in the coming ceremony. Thinking quickly, he had grabbed up the coal using his under-kimono instead. The shogun was amazed at his resourcefulness. That little page grew to become a great man—chief senior councilor Tanuma Okitsugu, who instituted monetary reform.

Anyone who would achieve great things must be able to pay close attention to little things and make quick judgments.

# 16

## "Watch Out for the Poisonous Snake"

*Treasure Brings Torment*

"Watch out for that poisonous snake. Don't let it bite you," said Buddha.

"I won't," said his disciple Ānanda, who was following close behind.

A farmer overheard this exchange and peered into the grass to see the dread creature for himself. What met his eyes instead was a glittering pile of silver and gold, half-buried in the ground. He muttered, "Someone must have buried this here long ago, and it got exposed by the rain. How foolish of the Buddha to mistake a pile of treasure for a poisonous snake!" He carried it home in glee.

In no time, the farmer's lifestyle grew so opulent that he became the talk of the land. His story eventually came to the attention of the king, who grew suspicious and subjected him to a strict cross-examination. The farmer confessed all. In appropriating such a vast treasure for himself he had committed a great crime, and he was promptly sentenced to death. He went home with just three days of grace. When his family heard what had happened, they were overcome with sorrow.

"Śākyamuni was right!" declared the farmer in heartfelt tones. "That treasure really was a poisonous snake. I got bitten by it and now I'm going to die—and the poison will affect even my wife and child. How much better if we could have gone on living together in peace and quiet! The treasure brought us nothing but torment."

The next day, a summons came from the king. Fearful that the execution had been moved up, the farmer presented himself at court in fear and trembling, only to be told he had been granted a full pardon. The king explained, "Before you went home, I had one of my men hide under the floorboards of your house. He heard the full story, from the words of Śākyamuni to your repentance. I thought it over and realized that you are not the only one to be bitten by that poisonous snake. Even I, who confiscated your treasure, was on the point of ruining the country with my decadence. I'll turn the treasure over to Śākyamuni for him to use."

When Śākyamuni heard all this, he smiled. "The treasure of this world often turns into an instrument of torture," he commented. "I'll use the silver and gold to spread teachings that lead one and all to true happiness."

Even prime ministers and heads of state are sometimes carted off to prison, tainted by the poison of greed and full of grief. No one is immune to the poisonous snake.

# 17

## Why Do Couples Quarrel?

One hot summer night, a husband comes home from work and greets his wife.

"I'm home, honey. Gosh, it's hot out there."

"Hi!" she says. "You must really have felt the heat. Even in the house it's sweltering, and you were out working all day long. Look at you, covered in sweat! Junior, go get a fan and cool Daddy off."

The husband puffs out his chest with pleasure. "Aw, it's nothing."

But what if the wife said this instead?

"It's summer, why shouldn't it be hot? You're not the only one who feels the heat, you know. But of course it's always about you."

Then he would respond: "You're in a lousy mood! As usual."

Men have two sides. Sometimes they are like generals reprimanding great armies, and other times they are like little boys in need of a hug. Sometimes a man is in full "follow me!" mode, and other times he wants nothing more than a relaxing head rub.

What happens when a husband hands his wife money?

"Here's a hundred bucks."

"Don't act like you're doing me a big favor. How much are you keeping back for yourself?"

"I need some to go out with the fellows after work. It's expected."

"You always say that. Why don't you come home and get sloshed instead of going out to bars?"

"And have to look at a face like a pig's bottom? That's enough to sober anyone."

"Ooh, I've put up with a lot from you, but that takes the cake. Seventeen years ago, who said 'If I can't be with you I'll *die*'?"

"Dammit, don't throw the past in my face!"

And on it goes.

Why do couples quarrel? Think of it this way: A husband and wife are joined by meshing gears with different numbers of teeth, as it were. It's inevitable that periodically the gears will get out of sync. When that happens, if one or the other says a simple "I'm sorry," the problem is resolved. If both resist, they stay at odds.

Trouble happens when couples think they are one in body and soul and so feel free to speak and behave rudely to each other. Keep in mind that your spouse is not you.

# 18

# Why the Navel Is in the Middle
# of the Body

Eyes see; ears hear; the nose smells; the mouth eats. Every part of the human body has an important role to play. Only the navel sits squarely in the middle with nothing to do. What's the use of having a navel, anyway?

Dogs, cats, and whales have navels; birds, fish, and frogs do not. The navel is a reminder of the time when we floated carefree in our mother's womb and the umbilical cord did all the work, absorbing nourishment. After birth the navel serves no purpose, but before we were born, it was literally of central importance. Without a navel, you would not exist. That's why the navel is centered in the body.

Picking at the navel or injuring it leads directly to a stomachache. Sometimes people abuse the elderly members of their family, criticizing them for being idle chatterboxes.

Families like that experience "stomachache" and, at some point, collapse. The elderly once did plenty of work, which is why they deserve a central place of honor in the home—just as the navel does in the body.

A landowner went to inspect his taro crop and found the rootstalks drooping. He pulled on one and lo and behold, it came up easily out of the ground. Someone had stolen all the corms and put the parent rootstalks back in place, then covered them over with dirt. It was a heartless thing to do.

Not only that, but the culprit had stuck a taunting sign in the ground: "I took the children. The parents are all yours."

Naturally the landowner had planted the parent rootstalks precisely because he wanted the "children"! Stung, he put up a bigger sign: "Take the parents. Leave the children to carry on the family."

Old people should gracefully relinquish the center stage, and watch over the next generation without saying too much. No one likes a navel that sticks out.

# 19

## "The Window Frame Hurts Too"

*A Winsome Mother and Child*

This happened once when I was riding a train on my way to give a speech. The car interior was spacious and quiet, with many unfilled seats. Feeling relaxed, I spread myself out and opened up a book I'd brought along. After a while, tired from reading and lulled by the rhythmical vibrations of the train, I began to nod off—only for my dreams to be shattered by an ear-splitting whistle and the metallic screech of brakes. Apparently the driver had found an obstruction of some kind at a crossing.

The shock of the sudden stop threw me forward, but I managed somehow to stay upright. In the same instant, the shrill sobs of a little child rang out. I saw then that the seats across the aisle in front of me were occupied by a young mother and her child, who had apparently been amusing himself by sitting with his forehead pressed against the windowpane, watching the scenery fly by. When the train jerked to a stop, the tot's head banged sharply into the window frame. His wails grew louder and more frantic. Afraid he was hurt, I jumped up, but to my relief there was no sign of injury. Then I witnessed a scene so heartwarming that I was deeply touched.

As the child's pain lessened, he gradually quieted down while his mother rubbed his head reassuringly and murmured soothing words: "Sweetheart, that must really hurt. I'm so sorry. I'll rub it for you and make the pain go away. But you know, you weren't the only one who got hurt. The poor window frame did too! Let's rub it and make it feel better, shall we?" The tot nodded, and sure enough, he and his mother together began to pat the window frame.

I felt ashamed of myself, for I had assumed she would say something more on these lines: "That must really hurt. I'm so sorry. It's all the fault of this naughty window frame. Let's spank it and teach it a lesson, shall we?" Such a scene is common enough, giving a toddler a vent for his rage and allowing the moment to pass.

All too often, when faced with difficulties, we cope by searching for someone else to blame for our suffering. Perhaps, I reflected, we parents implant this response in our children without meaning to. The child is father of the man, goes the saying, and surely parents have enormous influence in shaping the character of small children.

People who think only of themselves and cannot empathize with others, end in the darkness. The act of making others happy itself brings happiness. Those who would set their sights on the Pure Land must keep to the high road of benefiting others as well as themselves.

I left the train wishing true happiness to that mother and child with all my heart.

# 20

## Diamond Faith Is Stronger
## than the Sword

In 1496 the Shin Buddhist priest Rennyo built Honganji temple in Ishiyama, Settsu (today's Osaka Prefecture) in order to spread the teachings of the Shin founder, Shinran. People from all around gathered there in search of the truth, and Ishiyama prospered and grew, acquiring such power that the various lords could not ignore it.

Many years later, warlord Oda Nobunaga was quick to recognize the area's military and political importance, and he approached the temple many times with offers for the property. But that would have meant putting a Buddhist fortress, one protected with blood and tears since the time of Rennyo, into the hands of an enemy of Buddhism—someone who had burned down the temples on Mount

Hiei and killed thousands—an unthinkable prospect. Honganji naturally turned down the offers.

.

Finally in 1570 the insidious Nobunaga raised a great army to attack Ishiyama, but unexpectedly suffered a defeat that dealt a major blow to his army's morale. Generals opposed to Nobunaga also raised an army, forcing the stubborn attacker to withdraw for a time. He did not abandon his purpose, however.

In 1576 Nobunaga attacked three times from sea and land, but the fortress held firm; though it was defended by a militia, not samurai, the men fought with spirit. The mighty Nobunaga, despite the massive trained force at his command, suffered another great defeat. Men braced themselves for a return battle.

Nobunaga would not give up, but came back another four or five times to try to take the land by force. However, the citadel, a center of true Buddhism, was defended by people ready to lay down their lives to protect their faith. They refused to allow it to be trampled by enemy boots and horses' hooves.

Following his miraculous victory in the 1560 battle of Okehazama, Nobunaga had gone from strength to strength, adding daily to his territorial gains and sending five great warlords to defeat. Only in his attacks on Ishiyama was he forced to give up.

What was the source of the incredible strength of the Ishiyama defenders? A poem by a military leader of the times contains this line: "People are the fortress, the stone walls and the moat." In warding off an enemy attack, people's solidarity has far greater strength than any impregnable fortress built at whatever cost. The valiant fighters were helped by the lay of the land and by Nobunaga's powerful enemy, the Mori clan. But their greatest strength by far lay in the solidarity of their faith, faith that sprang from the truth of Amida's Vow and made the castle of truth as unyielding as adamantine.

The pen is mightier than the sword, they say. Mightier even than the pen is the power of faith.

# 21

## Never Remember a Kindness Done or Forget a Kindness Received

*William Tell*, playwright Friedrich Schiller's masterpiece, contains the following scene. In a mountain recess, Tell saves the life of his enemy the bailiff, then goes home and brags to his wife: "From now on the bailiff's attitude will surely change because of the debt he incurred today."

"You are deceiving yourself," warns his wife. "You will stick in his craw and he will resent you more than ever."

It often happens that while one person keeps track of kindnesses he has done, looking forward to a great return, the recipient of that same kindness struggles under the burden of debt and feels a mounting antipathy. Debtors are as likely as not to resent the very people who helped them.

This of course does not mean that there is no need for acts of kindness. The law of the universe is that you reap only what you sow. Good actions yield good results; bad actions bring bad results; and one's own actions determine one's fate. Good results cannot come about if good seeds are not planted, but attitude is crucial.

In the Japanese folktale "The Tongue-Cut Sparrow," an old man had a pet sparrow he was very fond of. One day when the old man was out, the sparrow ate up all his wife's starch. The old woman became so angry that she took out her scissors and snipped off the sparrow's tongue, rendering it mute. The poor sparrow flew off in tears. When the old man came home and heard what had happened, he was appalled at his wife's cruelty and set off to find his little friend. After a long, hard search, he finally found the sparrow and stayed the afternoon, happy to be together again. When it came time for him to go home, the sparrow offered him his choice of two wicker baskets, one large and one small. Without hesitation the old man picked the smaller one because it was lighter and easier to carry. When he got home, it turned out to be full of gold and jewels.

Seeing this, the old woman promptly set off to claim her own reward for "all she'd done to look after that sparrow."

Her heart was fixed on treasure, so when she was offered the same choice as her husband, she picked the larger basket, which turned out to be full of goblins and monsters.

The old man was content simply to be reunited with the pet sparrow he had searched for high and low; he asked nothing more. The old woman, on the other hand, thought to herself, "That sparrow owes me, because I took care of it." Her motive was not to comfort the sparrow—let alone to make amends for what she had done—but to acquire treasure. The goblins and monsters that set upon her in the end were the reflection of her own impure heart.

How pleasant it would be if people did all they could for one other without seeking anything in return! One should never remember a kindness done and never forget a kindness received.

# 22

## Success Is the Fruit of Effort
### *The Merchant's Fortitude*

Long ago, there were two merchants who always crossed a narrow mountain pass with dry goods loaded onto their backs.

One day, one of them plopped down on a rock by the roadside. "Exhausting, isn't it?" he sighed. "Let's rest for a while. If only this pass weren't so high, we could cross it easily and make more money. Right?" He looked up resentfully at the steep pass.

"I disagree," replied his companion. "In fact, I wish this pass were higher and steeper."

"You do?" said the first man in astonishment. "Whatever for? Do you enjoy suffering? How strange!"

His companion explained, "If this pass were easy to cross, everybody would use it to do business, and our profits would go down; if it were higher and steeper, no one but us would cross it, and our business would prosper even more."

Successful tradesmen must be not only astute in business, but bold in endeavor. Success is the fruit of one's effort. All that comes easily is poverty and shame.

The harder the task, the more glorious the triumph.

# 23

# "Those Who Feel No Gratitude Are Viler than Beasts"

A farmer was working in the field when he happened to come upon a tiny egg. He said to himself, "If I leave it here, it will be eaten by a dog or carried off by a bird. I'll take it home and try to hatch it."

During the day he put the egg in the sun, and at night he held it next to his skin to warm it. But when the egg hatched, to his surprise out came a tiny snake.

"Snakes are hated for being vindictive, but if I care sincerely for this little one, surely my feelings for it will get through." And so he resolved to bring up the snake.

He made the baby snake a nest, brought it soft food to eat, and did all he possibly could for its comfort. As the snake grew, it learned to understand most of what the farmer said, and did his bidding. Soon it learned to recognize his footsteps, and would come to the door to greet him on his return.

One night the farmer was invited out for dinner, and came home drunk. When he started to enter the house, his foot struck something and immediately he felt a searing flash of pain. He looked down and saw the snake.

"You ungrateful wretch!" he cried out in a fury. "After all I did for you, raising you from the time you were a bitty egg . . . how could you bite me!"

After a moment, however, he muttered quietly, "But come to think of it, I'm the one at fault. You came out to see me the way you always do. Even if I'm drunk, there was no call for me to forget all about you and trample you the way I did. Sudden pain made you bite the leg that hurt you. It's only natural. Forgive me."

Then he applied salve to the wound and went to bed.

In the morning he went to the snake's bed, but it was gone without a trace. He finally found it lying dead where it had bitten its master the night before, its own fangs sunk into its body.

Buddha taught, "The knowledge of gratitude is the basis of compassion and the gateway to good works. Those who feel no gratitude are viler than beasts."

Those who are grateful for the kindnesses they receive in life thrive. Those who take kindness for granted lose trust, and those who repay kindness with malice bring ruin upon themselves.

# 24

# "Doctor, Give Me a Dose
# of Poison!"

Once the eighteenth-century physician Goto Konzan was visited in the middle of the night by a young woman who had recently married into a merchant's family.

"Doctor," she said distractedly, "help me, for pity's sake! I have to have a dose of poison." The doctor sensed that something was very wrong.

"What for?" he asked.

"I want my mother-in-law to die."

The animosity between the two women was well known. Konzan gauged the situation and decided that if he refused her request, the desperate young woman might well take her own life.

"I see," he said. "Very well."

In a short time he handed her thirty packets of medicine, with this calm explanation. "If you poisoned her all at once, people would know right away. You would be crucified, and I would be beheaded. So here's what I want you to do. Give her one packet a night for thirty nights. I have adjusted the dosage so that on the thirtieth night she will drop dead."

The young woman thanked him with relief. As she started to leave, he added a word of advice. "You have only thirty more days to endure. During that time, I suggest you feed your mother-in-law her favorite foods, speak to her kindly, and massage her arms and legs."

From the following night on, the young woman did as Konzan had recommended. On the thirtieth night, she massaged her mother-in-law as usual. Afterwards, the old woman sat up, placed her hands on the floor and bowed her head low.

"My dear," she said, "I owe you an apology. I have been hard on you until now because I wanted you to learn the ways of our household quickly. This past month, you have been a different person. You have learned to show genuine consideration. I have nothing left to teach you. Starting tomorrow, I will step down and leave the household in your capable hands."

The young woman realized her mistake and rushed to Konzan's house, full of penitence. "Doctor," she implored tearfully, on her knees, "help me, for pity's sake! I have to have an antidote to the poison. Please make some right away!"

"Don't worry," said Konzan with a chuckle. "What I gave you was harmless, just buckwheat flour!"

# 25

## The Power of People Who Do Not
## Try to Impress Others

In mid-nineteenth-century Japan, a samurai named Yamada Asaemon served the government as executioner. One day he was asked by the famous swordsman Yamaoka Tesshu whether, in all the beheadings he had done, there had ever been a time when he missed.

"I worried when I beheaded famous men like Yoshida Shoin,"* answered the executioner, "but perhaps out of pride they all held themselves rigid, so there was no difficulty. Two other times, I did have trouble." One botched execution was that of Jirokichi the Rat, the celebrated thief who stole from the rich and gave to the poor, he said. The other was that of the famous Yoshiwara courtesan Kacho, a convicted arsonist.

---

* 1830–59. A charismatic intellectual and revolutionary in the years leading to the Meiji Restoration of 1868.

Jirokichi must have accepted that after years of daring thievery, the time for atonement had come. He calmly faced west and said, "Please do it." He looked and sounded perfectly natural.

Kacho came to the block wearing little makeup, her palms pressed together in devotion, her figure so natural that even "Decapitator Asaemon," as he was known, could scarcely bring himself to lower the sword. Despite his expertise, he missed the spot time and again; it took him five tries to properly sever her head.

Nothing is so hard to deal with in others, it seems, as a complete lack of intention to impress.

One day the great Saigo Takamori, dressed in his general's uniform, was climbing a steep hill with some young officers. At the same time, a coolie was struggling to pull a heavy load up the hill. The incline was so steep that he couldn't budge the cart. Worse, the cart was on the point of slipping back down. When he saw this, without hesitation Saigo ordered his men to come help him push the cart. They all joined forces and succeeded in getting the cart to the top of the hill. The grateful coolie thanked them profusely before going on his way.

One of the young officers commented, "Some people would laugh to see a general in the army pushing a cart like that."

"Yes," said Saigo, "but that's nothing to me. I never care what people say. They can say whatever they want!" Then he gave a ringing laugh.

Saigo Takamori—who later played an important role in the movement to overthrow the shogunate, and took Edo Castle without bloodshed—stuck to his principles and pursued his beliefs without trying to impress anyone, paying no attention to what others thought. That is how he was able to live up to the faith and aspirations of his countrymen and devote his life to the welfare of his country.

# 26

## "Your Mother Is Precious Because She Devoted Her Life to Raising You"

Once there was a young bride who earnestly pursued Buddhism.

One summer's evening during a wild thunderstorm, her mother-in-law, a widow whose husband had been killed by lightning, sat alone cowering inside her mosquito net. Concerned about the older woman, who she knew was deathly afraid of thunder and lightning, the young woman came downstairs, pushed her way inside the mosquito net, and held the other woman tightly to comfort her.

"You should be safe in here," she told her. "The net is made of hemp, which doesn't conduct electricity. And even if we were to die tonight, I would be right beside you." When his wife didn't come back, the young man wondered what had happened to her and went downstairs to find her.

He was moved to see her sitting with her arms around his mother.

Later, back upstairs, he asked his wife, "Does my mother mean that much to you?"

She replied, "You are more precious to me than anything in the world. And your mother, since she devoted her life to raising you, is just as precious."

Fortunate the family that can welcome such a daughter-in-law. Fortunate the husband who is blessed with such a wife.

# 27

## All Things Come to an End

This happened when Ikkyu, the famously clever Zen monk, was an acolyte of seven or eight. One day after the head priest had stepped out for a while, Ikkyu visited his room and found another acolyte there, crying his eyes out.

"What's wrong?" asked Ikkyu.

"You know that antique tea bowl that was a gift from the shogun, the one the master likes to show off to guests? I wanted to see it, so I took it out of the box and was admiring it when I dropped it and . . . it broke!" He held up the two halves of the bowl, sobbing.

"That's all you're upset about?" said Ikkyu. "It's too bad, but there's no point in crying. Don't forget, you're studying to be a Zen priest. You mustn't fall apart over a little thing like a broken dish. Have some pride—a Zen priest shouldn't cry. If tears could put the tea bowl back together then you could cry all you liked, but since they won't, why don't you stop all that noise?"

"Is that all you can say?" wailed the other boy. "Of course crying doesn't help, I know. But that just makes me cry even more. Have a heart!"

"Cheer up," said Ikkyu. "We disciples have to stick together. I'll see what I can do. How's this? I'll say I'm the one who broke it. Now you don't have to cry, do you?"

"Would you really do that for me? Thanks! You're so smart, Ikkyu, I'm sure you can figure out a way to make the master calm down. If you do, I promise I'll give you all my bean-jam buns from now on!"

And so, with a promise of bean-jam buns that might or might not materialize, Ikkyu agreed to take the blame. He stuck the broken pieces carelessly in the sleeve of his kimono, went straight to the lecture hall, and played games as usual.

In the evening when the head priest returned, Ikkyu went out to greet him with the rest. Catching sight of his star pupil, the older man beamed and called out, "Well, Ikkyu, what mischief have you been up to today?"

"None, Master. I was in the lecture hall all day, meditating on a koan."

"A likely story. I'll bet you were napping."

"No, Master. I meditated with all my might, but there was one problem I couldn't solve."

"What is it? Tell me."

"All right. My question is, must all people die, or not? What is the truth concerning birth and death?"

"Well, you're a bright boy, but you're still young. Here, I'll explain it for you. The Buddha taught us that everyone who is born must die. No one can escape death—not even Buddha himself, nor any hero who ever lived."

"Death is that powerful?" replied Ikkyu. "I see. That's one problem solved. Thank you."

"Is there something else?"

"Yes. My other question is, do all things in this world come to an end, or not? What is the truth concerning being and nonbeing of the things in this world?"

"Bright or not, what a child you are, to be fretting about such things. I'll tell you exactly how it is: everything in this world is doomed to perish. Buddha taught us that. Keep it well in mind."

"But Master," pursued Ikkyu, "what if something is very precious, and we take extra special care of it? Then won't it last forever?"

"No. No matter how careful we are, everything comes to an end when its time comes."

"I see! So time, too, is very powerful."

"Yes, indeed. Not even Buddha could stop time or alter its effects."

"Thanks to you, Master, all the problems I struggled with today have been cleared up. Those who are born must die, and everything that has form must come to an end. These are the great truths of the universe."

"That's right. They are unchanging laws."

"So even if someone important to you dies, you shouldn't weep or wail in sorrow, and even if an object important to you is broken, you shouldn't get angry and carry on. In either case, you should accept that it was time for that to happen, and let go without regret. That is true enlightenment, isn't it?"

"Yes. You've got it."

"I certainly am lucky to have one so enlightened as my master."

"Now, now. Flattery will get you nowhere. I'm not giving you anything, so don't fish."

"No, master. But I have something to give you."

Calmly Ikkyu pulled out the broken pieces of the prized tea bowl.

"Here is something whose time had come."

The head priest was taken aback, but after all he had just said he could hardly administer a scolding.

His only comment was a bemused, "I see. Its time had come, all right."

# 28

## The Tone of the Instrument Depends on the Player, Not on the Price

News of that day's concert raised a stir, for the famous virtuoso was to perform on a violin valued at five thousand dollars—a fortune at the time. The violinist took the stage to a thundering ovation. "Look!" cried an awestruck voice in the audience. "There it is!" The crowd gaped at the instrument in the maestro's hand.

Finally the concert began. Sublime music, now quick in tempo and now slow, poured out of the violin and entranced the listeners. "What a wonderful tone," sighed one. "It sounds like a million dollars," said another. "What I wouldn't give to be able to play such a violin myself!" Up and down the hall, people expressed their admiration in similar language.

In the middle of the sixth piece on the program, the

music came to a sudden stop. The maestro took his violin and slammed it over a chair, smashing it to pieces. Shocked, the audience rose to its feet.

The evening's host came out on stage with a replacement violin and urged the audience to stay calm. "The violin that was just destroyed was an ordinary cheap one. Too many musicians nowadays take pride in how much their instrument cost. No one regrets this tendency more than the maestro. He wants to impress a simple truth on the world: the tone of a violin depends not on how much it cost, but on who plays it. The violin that he will now use is the one that cost five thousand dollars."

The music started up again and enraptured its listeners once again, ending to a storm of applause and cries of "Encore!" The audience that day never could tell any difference between the cheap instrument and the five-thousand-dollar one.

# 29

# Despite Surface Differences,
# We Are All the Same

The human body is made up of various organs and parts: eyes, nose, mouth, ears, limbs. No matter how busy the hands may be, the feet do not help out, and no matter how overworked the eyes may be, the ears do not pitch in. Eyes are eyes and ears, ears; each one operates within its natural zone. That is what keeps the body working smoothly.

If a mosquito lands on a toe, the hand swiftly acts to keep the toe from being bitten. The eye measures where the mosquito is, and the hand delivers a smart slap. In this way, when an emergency arises all the parts work together to protect the life of the whole.

Nature offers other examples of unity and differentiation. Rain falls equally on all vegetation, without discriminating according to size. Large trees absorb large amounts of rainwater, small ones absorb small amounts. What if all plants, large and small, took in equal portions of water? Some would die from too much moisture, others from too little. Rain falls equally on all, and plants thrive equally by absorbing the life-giving rain in unequal measure.

Just think how full of inequality society is! Human beings come in an infinite diversity of rich and poor, intelligent and unintelligent, talented and untalented. People gloating over a high government position or scrambling along the road to success or hauling their earnings to the bank. People burdened with sickness or handicaps. People taking the wrong path in life, slaves to lust. Once-healthy people lying bedridden and paralyzed, treated as encumbrances. People weeping over a failed marriage or a burned-down home, utterly bereft, not knowing which way to turn.

Elegantly dressed people may seem to exist on a higher plane, without mundane physical needs. The idea of a finely dressed lady squatting on the toilet or a gentleman in tuxedo relieving himself may seem vaguely incongruous, but it shouldn't. The problem lies in seeing these surface differences as real differences.

We may look different, but we are all merely players on the stage of life, each one playing his part. Once we are finished playing our role and go backstage, we are all the same.

# 30

## Resolution in the Face of Death

Once long ago there was a quiet man who, though a member of the samurai warrior caste, had neither grounding in swordsmanship nor courage in battle. Who should he encounter one day but a fierce warrior bent on racking up one hundred victims, who challenged him to a showdown. For a samurai to refuse such a challenge was unthinkable. Not knowing what else to do, the man asked for time to see to his lord's affairs, and used the reprieve to visit a nearby master swordsman. After explaining the situation in full, he asked what to expect in the conflict and how he should prepare to meet his death by the sword.

Impressed by the level of his determination, the master carefully instructed him in everything from the etiquette of dueling to the proper way of folding his kimono. Finally he taught him the art of *aiuchi*, a deadly mutual attack. Yield to your opponent and in return, strike home. In so doing you sacrifice your own life, but unfailingly end your enemy's life as well.

"Start with an attack stance five or six steps in front of your opponent, holding the sword high over your head. Then slowly close your eyes and open your mind's eye, waiting with undivided attention for him to strike. The moment you sense the spirit of his sword awaken, bring your weapon down with all your might. In this way you may be killed, but your opponent will surely be split in twain."

The samurai thanked the master deeply and proceeded to the site of the duel, where his challenger was awaiting him. Now prepared for what would come, the samurai followed to the letter the teachings he had been given. He carefully folded his kimono, strode boldly forward and took up the attack stance, then trained all his attention on his opponent, his mind focused on discovering his chance. Yet the challenger gave no sign of striking, and the spirit of the sword was dormant. Finally, above the murmurs of the crowd that had gathered to watch, the samurai heard the cry "I surrender!" and opened his eyes in surprise.

"Clearly, your skill is far above mine," the humbled challenger said. "The energy that emanates from your center, the perfection of your stance . . . please teach me the secrets of your art." Covered with the greasy sweat of fear, he prostrated himself on the ground.

Nothing is more powerful than resolution in the face of death. He who willingly pours his life's blood into the task at hand will find a way.

# 31

## Constantly Polish Yourself

*More suffering is
always just around the corner.
Because it is everywhere,
you can constantly
polish yourself.*

# 32

## Step Back and Look Again

*Take a step back*
*and look from an outsider's view at*
*yourself and your suffering.*
*Then you will see*
*it's not as bad as you thought.*

# 33

## On Self-destruction

*How foolish we human beings are!*
*Despite knowing better,*
*we let ourselves be destroyed*
*by things like pride, stubbornness,*
*and desire for fame and wealth.*

# 34

## On Wrong Efforts

*Effort expended on going*
*in the wrong direction*
*is wasted.*
*First take the time to think hard*
*about which way you should go.*
*Make sure you're headed in the right way,*
*and then go full tilt.*

# 35

## On Saying "Thank You"

*We all think we strive harder than anyone else. It makes us angry to see others sailing along without any difficulties. But in fact we ourselves are the ones who have it easiest, while others struggle with their backs to the wall. Our inability to see this keeps us from feeling gratitude, keeps us from saying a simple "thank you."*

# 36

## Seeds That Are Planted

*It's only a question of time.*
*Sooner or later,*
*the circle of truth spreads*
*everywhere.*

# 37

## Hurry Up and Be Patient

*The law of cause and effect holds true*
*throughout the universe.*
*Until cause and condition come together,*
*the effect will not emerge.*
*It's important to wait patiently*
*until then.*
*Hurry up and plant the seeds, and then wait*
*without any impatience.*

# 38

## On Avoiding Ups and Downs

*Many people despair over a single scolding,*
*thinking all is lost.*
*Many people preen over a single compliment,*
*thinking all is well.*

# 39

## Gauging the Moment

*"Now!"*
*When the moment comes,*
*you must act with resolve.*
*It's difficult to*
*gauge the right moment*
*and be decisive.*

# 40

## Why Is Life Precious?

*Why is human life infinitely precious?*
*Why should I be glad I was born*
*a human being?*
*Why must I show respect to my parents?*
*Can you give clear answers?*

# 41

## On Tunnel Diggers

*The ones who dug this tunnel sure*
*had it rough.*
*We have it easy.*
*All we do is pass through—whoosh!*

# 42

## On Misunderstanding

*Life is full of misunderstanding.*
*When misunderstanding*
*is resolved,*
*closer trust is born.*

# 43

## On Thinking of Tomorrow Today

*We are often told, "Don't put off till tomorrow what you should do today." But in fact taking care of today's business is not enough. We must also try today to do what we can about tomorrow. Succumbing to panic as one lies near death does no good. By then it is too late.*

# 44

## On Buying Things

*Don't haggle too much.*
*Let the seller make a profit.*
*Even if you walk away with a bargain,*
*the seller's look of disappointment*
*spoils things.*
*Both sides should end up satisfied.*

# 45

## On Lost Love

*If the one you love leaves you for another,*
*what should you do?*
*Many people are shocked and lose heart, but*
*that's no good.*
*Try to better yourself.*
*Make them sorry they didn't marry you.*

# 46

## The Need for Balance

*Gentleness alone isn't enough.*
*Strictness alone is no good.*

# 47

## On Truth

*What must be made clear is*
*the truth.*
*Nothing else.*

# 48

## Bonds from the Distant Past

*We are surprised because we see*
*only this world.*
*Things happen through ties*
*with Buddhism*
*extending back untold aeons.*

# 49

## On the Path of Suffering

*Unless we take the path of suffering
—the one that hardly anyone chooses—
we cannot shine.*

# 50

## What Brings Success

*Success comes*
*by making efforts that no one else does.*

# 51

## On the Solemnity of Truth

*Truth has no relation to human thought*
*or convenience.*
*Whether we accept the truth or not,*
*whether it amazes us or not,*
*whether we feel right about it or not,*
*whether it suits our convenience or not*
*—none of this has any bearing on the truth.*
*Herein lies its solemnity.*

# 52

## The Secret

*In all things, self-reflection is key.*

# 53

## The Man Capable of Doing Great Work

In the age of Alexander the Great, there lived a philosopher named Diogenēs. While Alexander the Great sought world conquest, Diogenēs was an itinerant philosopher who slept in a tub and appeared now in town, now in villages, leading people to virtue. Alexander heard about him and was impressed. He sent for him, intending to give him a reward.

Diogenēs promptly turned the invitation down. "I have no business with the king. If he has business with me, let him come and see me."

And so Alexander called on Diogenēs. "Thank you for guiding the people of this country," he said. "Tell me what you want, and I promise I will fulfill your wish."

Diogenēs had been basking pleasurably in the sunlight.

"I'll tell you what I want," he said. "I want you to get out of the way. You're blocking my sunlight."

The power of Alexander the Great meant nothing to Diogenēs.

Centuries ago, a luxurious culture thrived in the domain of Kaga, north of Kyoto in Japan. The ruler of Kaga heard of the fame of the haiku poet Kobayashi Issa and ordered his retainer to have the poet write a verse for him. The retainer went to Issa's residence with a sheet of paper. The unimpressed poet spat into his inkstone and ground some ink, then with a broken-tipped brush wrote out these words:

> What's the big deal?
> Even the glory of Kaga
> is dew on the grass.

"Nothing is so hard to deal with as a man who clings to neither money nor status nor position nor life. But only a man like that is capable of doing great work." Those were the words of the rebel and statesman Saigo Takamori.

# 54

# What Is the Best Legacy to Our Children?

Three scholars were leaving to pursue their studies abroad. An uneducated fellow wished to accompany them, so they took him along as porter. The foursome crossed mountains and forded rivers, coming eventually to a desert strewn with the bones of a wild beast.

"Let's test our skill, shall we?" said the three. They gathered the bones and began to fit them back together, using all their ingenuity.

"If the beast comes back to life, won't it devour you?" fretted the porter.

"You don't know anything," the scholars barked at him. "Be quiet and watch!" They proceeded to add flesh and hide to the assembled skeleton, until lo and behold there stood a strapping lion.

The uneducated porter had by now climbed a tree in terror. Holding his breath, he watched as the wise men breathed life into the lion. With flashing eye and bared fang, it devoured the three and ran off.

A world-famous professor at Harvard University was so busy with other work that he had no time to attend his own class. He recorded his lectures and instructed his students to gather once a week to listen to the tapes. One day he happened to pass by the door of his classroom and looked inside. On a desk in the center of the room a tape recorder was whirring away, surrounded by desks bearing smaller tape recorders.

When children come home from school, tiger moms pounce: "How did you do on the test? Hurry up now, your private tutor is waiting for you." Some parents misguidedly place so much emphasis on their children's intellectual development that they end up using up all their savings and even selling their home. Thrown into a living nightmare, they hold desperate family councils.

Sometimes parents who chase after a college education for their children end up being eaten alive by a monster. Ungrateful children who are moral failures do not bring their parents pride, but eat up their money and break their hearts. Moral education—education that cultivates the heart—is most important.

Providing children with a material legacy is the low way. Providing them with an academic education is the medium way. Aim high by giving your children moral education.

It is important not to lose sight of what constitutes true parental love.

# 55

# The Wisdom and Strength of Will to "Slay Ma Su, Shedding Tears"

The end of the Chinese Han Dynasty was a turbulent time that produced many larger-than-life figures. Sun Quan, the ruler of Wu, and Cao Cao, the lord of Wei, each acquired great strength, together splitting the realm virtually in half. One other hero, Liu Bei, was squeezed into a small area between them, under constant pressure.

Liu Bei's eye fell on the brilliant military strategist Zhuge Liang, who was then living in reclusion, farming in fine weather and studying when it rained, enjoying a life of dignified leisure far removed from the chaos of the times. Three times Liu Bei called at Zhuge Liang's residence in hopes of recruiting him. Won over by this demonstration of respect and sincerity, Zhuge Liang became his devoted advisor and, with great savvy and adroitness, succeeded in establishing the kingdom of Shu. Thus began what we know as the period of the Three Kingdoms, with Shu, Wu, and Wei locked in a three-way rivalry.

Liu Bei, the founding emperor of Shu, died without having achieved his full intent. He was succeeded by his son, Liu Shan. In order to carry out his late lord's wishes, Zhuge Liang stayed on to help the new emperor and lead a campaign to subjugate the kingdom of Wei. However, he was hard-pressed, because he knew that his army was not strong enough to defeat Wei, and because he would be leaving the young and inexperienced Liu Shan on the throne.

Facing battle against his country's great rival, Zhuge Liang did not know if he would return dead or alive. And so before leaving he wrote a memorial to the young emperor that contained a detailed explanation of political affairs. That is the famous "Memorial on Dispatching the Troops," a document of such sincerity and insight that no one, they say, can read it dry-eyed.

Zhuge Liang then set off, seizing Qishan and occupying Nan'an, Tianshui, and Anding in quick succession.

Then Ma Su, a general of whom Zhuge Liang was

extremely fond, disobeyed orders and caused a huge defeat. To enforce discipline, Zhuge Liang resolved that his beloved general must pay the penalty for his actions, and ordered his execution.

That is the origin of the saying "slay Ma Su, shedding tears," meaning "to punish a subordinate for wrongdoing, regardless of personal connection or feelings."

He who would accomplish great things must possess the wisdom and strength of will to be able to act against his own personal feelings.

# 56

## Let the Slanderers Talk

Back in eighteenth-century Japan, the pretty, popular, un-married daughter of a saké merchant became pregnant. As her condition began to show, the news spread like wildfire, and her father badgered her mercilessly to name who had done this to her. Afraid to tell the truth, the girl thought in desperation that if she pointed a finger at the saintly Zen priest Hakuin, whose temple was nearby, that might get her off the hook. She whispered to her mother, "Actually, the child I am carrying is from Hakuin."

When her father heard this, he became enraged and barged into the temple without removing his shoes. He demanded to see the eminent priest, and directed a barrage of curses and insults at him. Then, his anger still unappeased, he demanded a sum of money to help defray childcare expenses.

Hakuin's response was classic. "Ah, I see," he said, and handed the irate father a slight amount of money.

People who had previously dismissed the accusation now became convinced that it was true, and Hakuin was indeed a hypocrite. This gossip, too, spread far and wide in no time. Hakuin paid no heed to the appalling things that were said about him. His policy was "Let the slanderer commit slander; let people have their say. It is for others to speak and for me to accept or reject what is said."

Tortured by the unexpected storm she had stirred up, the girl finally was forced to tell her parents the truth. Now they were doubly astonished. They marched her straight to the temple, where the three prostrated themselves and apologized over and over for their unpardonable behavior.

"Ah, I see." Once again Hakuin said only this, nodding.

Though we may be living upright lives, sometimes it happens that unfounded slander and gossip take us by surprise, filling us with anguish and anger. But in time the facts will emerge, resonating far and wide like the sound of a drum in the hands of a master.

In past, present, and future

there is none whom everyone slanders,

none who is praised by all.

—Wisdom of the Buddha (The Dhamma-pada)

# 57

## "My Life You May Have, But Not My Money!"
### *The Words That Scared Off a Legendary Bandit*

Once there was a hardworking grocer. He had a large sum of money, and was so worried about someone stealing it that he could barely sleep at night.

One night a buddha came to him in a dream and announced: "Before long a well-known thief will come by. Tell him plainly, 'My life you may have, but not my money.' If you do that, all will be well."

The grocer woke up in a cold sweat.

Eventually, just as the buddha had said, he was visited by a thief. "Look, you," said the thief gruffly, "if you want to live, hand over your money!" The grocer remembered what he had dreamed and said sharply, "My life you may have, but not my money!" The thief ran off in fear and disappeared.

Eventually, when the legendary bandit Ishikawa Goemon

was apprehended, he looked back on this episode and confessed, "Never in my life did I ever hear any words so terrifying."

There is nothing that cannot be done if you stake your life on it.

> When the petal falls
> is when it floats—
> lotus blossom

> The force of its entry
> propels it from the water again—
> frog in a pond.

# 58

## "Wear Fine Clothes, Eat Fine Food, and Do Your Makeup Every Day"

The wife of a millionaire was renowned for her wisdom, and the couple's only daughter was said to be a very sensible young woman as well. The wife of a high government official suggested that she would make their only son a wonderful wife, and in due course the young people were betrothed.

Not long before the wedding, the official's wife called at the home of the bride-to-be and overhead the following maternal advice being given in earnest tones: "Now dear, remember what I always tell you. When you are married, be sure to wear fine clothes, eat fine food, and do your makeup every day."

What kind of frivolous creature is joining our family,

the official's wife thought in dismay. It was too late to cancel the nuptials. She went home with strong misgivings.

The wedding took place without incident, but in the days following the official's wife, worried about what was to come, kept a wary eye on her new daughter-in-law. Yet to her surprise and pleasure, the young bride never failed to get up early to clean the house, sweep the garden, and do the wash, besides looking after her husband and father-in-law and keeping the kitchen sparkling clean. She showed no sign of frivolity.

At last the older woman's curiosity got the best of her. "Your mother told you that after you married you should wear fine clothes, eat fine food, and do your makeup, but you haven't done any such thing, have you?"

"Please, let me explain," said the bride. "By 'wear fine clothes' Mother meant 'always be cleanly in your appearance.' By 'eat fine food' she meant 'work hard,' because hard work makes everything taste good. And by 'do your makeup' she meant for me to keep the house clean and tidy, inside and out." She said this with a radiant smile.

The official's wife could only marvel at the excellent training the girl's mother had given her. Love of cleanliness is indeed a virtue in all.

# 59

## They Fought Like Tigers Because They
## Were Cornered

Han Xin was a brilliant Chinese general of ancient times. In the year 204 BCE, he broke through defenses on the Yellow River and attacked the lands of Wei and Dai. He captured alive the king of Wei and the Dai prime minister Xia Shuo and then, piling victory on victory, swept on to the kingdom of Zhao.

Chen Yu, the Zhao general, was undismayed. "No matter how strong Han Xin's forces may be, he has only a few thousand men. Besides, they are a thousand leagues from home, exhausted. We'll take them on and win in one blow." He lay in wait for Han Xin with a massive army of two hundred thousand.

Though accurate in his assessment, Chen Yu overlooked

one thing: Han Xin's genius in deploying troops. That was the mistake of his lifetime.

Han Xin had his troops cross the river so that they would be fighting with their backs to it, literally burning their bridges behind them. When the Zhao general saw this from afar, he laughed in scorn, as the plan violated a basic principle of warfare. Common sense dictated that an army fighting defensively by a river should camp on the side away from the enemy so that the river would be an obstacle reducing the enemy's strength.

The Zhao army attacked in full force. But with the river at their backs and nowhere to go, Han Xin's army fought ferociously, and the tide of battle turned against the Zhao. As they were withdrawing temporarily, Han Xin boxed them in and wiped them out. Chen Yu was killed and Prince Zhao Xie was captured.

The following day, Han Xin was asked why he had adopted such an unorthodox tactic. "It is true that by camping with the river at our backs we cut off our own escape route. It is an extremely dangerous tactic, but that way the soldiers fight for dear life. My regulars had all been sent home, and I was fighting with new soldiers mustered in occupied lands—a motley bunch, unfortunately. Without the river at their backs, I was afraid they would all turn tail and run. I had no choice but to put them where I did. They fought like tigers because they were cornered, and that's how they were able to annihilate the Zhao army that had seemed so invincible."

All the generals present were deeply impressed.

Resolution in the face of death opens a way.

# 60

## The Wise Man Learns
## from Everyone

In ancient times, the great Chinese military general Han Xin pulled off the astounding exploit of defeating, in a two-month span, the kingdoms of Wei and Dai as well as Zhao and Yan. He is famous for the tactic of placing his troops in front of a river, forcing them to fight hard to overcome a situation from which there was no other escape. Another time he won a bloodless victory by according a defeated general favorable treatment.

Han Xin's defeat of the Zhao forces, which were ten times the strength of his, gave him the momentum to ride on to attack Yan. On the way, he loosened the bonds of the captured general Li Zuoche and, paying him proper deference, asked his advice. He did so because he had long had the highest respect for the other man's judgment.

At first Li Zuoche adamantly declined, saying, "Defeated generals should not talk of battles," but at Han Xin's repeated insistence, he finally opened up.

"Following your success in crossing the Yellow River to attack, you defeated the kingdoms of Wei and Dai. Now that you have defeated our great Zhao army as well, and taken the king and myself captive, your fame resounds in every corner of the land. But the fact is, your soldiers are exhausted from these endless battles in far-off lands, and their fighting ability is at a low ebb. Take this tired army of yours to the strong fortress of Yan now and you will only face a long, drawn-out battle, without being able to take the castle. Not only will you fail to achieve your goal, but you will endanger your own life."

After delivering this warning, he added, "What you should do is rest your men and let them return to full fighting strength. Then if you dispatch your army to the border and send the leaders of Yan a simple threat, they will be so intimidated by your recent string of victories that they will do whatever you say. Once they have capitulated, send an eloquent spokesman to the country of Qi, and it will surrender, too. That way, the whole world will be at your feet."

Han Xin took this wise advice, and within the month he defeated Yan without bloodshed.

The foolish man learns from no one, but the wise man can learn from any quarter.

# 61

## Reliable Beauty

*Śākyamuni's Lecture to a Young Beauty*

Jetavana-vihāra, a renowned temple in India where Śākyamuni Buddha taught, was founded by a wealthy man named Anāthapiṇḍada. In time Anāthapiṇḍada married his only son to a beautiful girl, one so lovely that she was known as Sujātā. But Sujātā was so caught up in her own beauty that she felt she had done the family a favor by marrying into it and so turned a deaf ear to everything her husband and parents-in-law said.

In desperation, Anāthapiṇḍada and his wife turned to Śākyamuni, whom they had long revered, for help. "Please," they begged, "do something to improve her attitude!"

Śākyamuni was deeply sympathetic to their plight. Early the next morning, he set off for Anāthapiṇḍada's house with a large number of his disciples. Everyone else came out to greet the visitors respectfully, but Sujātā alone remained in an inner chamber and perversely refused to come out.

Śākyamuni read her mind, and with his mysterious power changed all the walls of the house to glass. Sujātā was caught by surprise. She had thought no one would find her hiding in an inner closet, but suddenly she was visible from all directions and could no longer stay hidden. She came running out and knelt before Śākyamuni, who spoke gently to her.

"Sujātā, no matter how beautiful a woman's face and figure may be, if her heart is corrupt she is hideous. Shiny black hair one day turns white, and pearly teeth fall out. Faces grow wrinkled, limbs lose their mobility, and that's not all: once the wind of transience has blown over us, our form changes into a dreadfully pitiable state. What is there to be proud of in such a body? Don't you think it's more important to strive instead to become a woman with a beautiful heart, one whom everyone holds dear?"

Then he spoke with her at length about the seven different types of wives in the world, and asked, "Which type do you want to be?"

Sujātā was thoroughly penitent and became a model of womanhood for later ages. And with peace and harmony restored, Anāthapiṇḍada's family prospered all the more.

# 62

## We Sweep and Sweep But Leaves Keep Falling

A man called on an eminent monk, bowing respectfully as he said, "I am a physician. Starting with the death of my wife I have suffered a series of setbacks, and life has become intolerable. I want to become a monk and purify my mind. Please let me be your disciple."

"Your intention is worthy," replied the old monk, "but I am in no position to take on any disciples."

"I have come in respect for your renown. Please hear my request."

Seeing the strength of his visitor's resolve, the old monk said quietly, "Will you do whatever I tell you to do?"

"Yes. I will obey you unconditionally."

"Fine. Then get a broom and sweep up the leaves on the ground."

"Yes, master."

It was late fall, and leaves were scattering in a drizzling rain. The physician quickly set to sweeping up leaves with great concentration, getting soaked in the rain. The monk never told him to stop, but only looked on steadily as he worked.

After a while the physician asked, "Shall I go on sweeping?"

"You still don't get it?" the monk shouted.

"Get what?" The physician thought hard, but he had no idea what he was failing to understand. In the meantime it was getting dark out, and the rain was coming down harder. Finally he became exhausted and asked for an explanation.

"Listen," said the monk. "You sweep as hard as you can, and what happens? Leaves keep right on falling, and the ground is never swept clean. Your wanting to enter the priesthood to purify your mind is the same. However we try to sweep away the dust of our blind passions, it will never disappear. Rather than abandoning the world, take that same determination and use it to heal people with your medical skill."

The man's eyes were opened, and he became a trusted doctor, widely praised for his skill and compassion.

Some things are possible, others not. Until we try, we don't know whether or not a thing is possible. It is only by applying ourselves with sincerity that we learn what we can and cannot do.

Believing something is impossible when it's not is sheer laziness. It requires wisdom to see clearly that what cannot be done, cannot be done.

# 63

## What It Takes to Turn Defeat
## to Victory

In war, sometimes an unexpected move can turn defeat into victory.

In a surprise military attack, the commander seizes his chance and leads a relatively small number of men against a large enemy force. If the enemy commander stays cool and collected, the risk of failure is great, but if the tactic succeeds, the enemy forces will be routed, fleeing in disarray without putting up a fight.

The twelfth-century general Minamoto Yoshitsune was a master of the surprise attack. With his brother Yoritomo, he defeated the rival Taira clan twice, first in 1184 at the battle of Ichinotani and then the next year at Yashima on the island of Shikoku, finally destroying them in 1185 at the battle of Dannoura. His battle tactics were breathtakingly reckless. At Ichinotani, his strategist remonstrated with him, saying, "The art of war knows no such rashness." But Yoshitsune turned a deaf ear and rode straight down a steep cliff, attacking the Taira camp from behind and putting the enemy to rout. At Dannoura he famously escaped by jumping from ship to ship, eight in all, agilely dodging his pursuers. Even allowing for exaggeration, that is not how a military commander is "supposed" to behave.

In the battle of Midway, which turned the tide of World War II, the Japanese Combined Fleet had the advantage over the United States Pacific Fleet in both numbers and training. Why then did it suffer a disastrous defeat? Risk-taking by the American commanders was a decisive factor.

Throughout the naval war, successful American surprise attacks contributed to victory.

Admiral Chester Nimitz of the battle of Midway, Rear Admiral Frank Fletcher of the battle of the Coral Sea, Vice Admiral William Halsey of the battle of the Santa Cruz Islands, and Admiral Raymond Spruance of the battle of the Philippine Sea were all daredevils, not military experts trained to be prudent. Spruance and Halsey were actually looked down upon by those who went strictly by the book.

Similarly, Japanese Admiral Togo Heihachiro, who clinched a great victory in the Russo-Japanese War, was until the war an undistinguished vice admiral, not a member of the military elite. Precisely because he was not a "model student," he was able to execute a daring U-turn in the face of the oncoming Russian fleet, a move that led to Japan's decisive victory.

Bright people who learn their lessons too well and always go by the book, afraid to try anything different, are not cut out to pull off a victory by surprise attack.

# 64

## Make Light of the Small and Lose the Great

Railroad executive James Hill, whose Great Northern Railway was completed in 1893, arrived one day in the ritzy Seattle Hotel in the state of Washington. He soon sent orders for the entire hotel staff to gather in the lobby. Everyone was excited at the prospect of receiving a fat tip from the newly rich chief executive.

Soon the beaming Hill appeared. "Today I will be staying in this hotel. I wanted to give each of you a little something to mark the start of our relationship, but unfortunately I do not have sufficient cash with me. Please accept this small token of my appreciation. I will be back in two weeks, so keep it carefully until then." He proceeded to hand each worker a fifty-cent coin made of nickel.

People's hopes having been high, their disappointment

was correspondingly great. The bellhops sneered or fumed; some went so far as to hurl their coin out the window. Most people spent their fifty cents on tobacco or the bathhouse before the week was out.

When Hill returned as promised two weeks later, he assembled the hundred-odd staff in the lobby again. "If you still have the nickel coin I gave you the other day, please speak up. I will exchange it now for a five-dollar gold coin."

When one young man who had scrupulously followed Hill's instructions handed over his coin, Hill turned it over and checked it before replacing it with a five-dollar coin. Two or three other youths exchanged glances and then fished nickel coins from their wallets. But Hill said, "The coins I handed out have a special mark on them. These do not. Does anyone else have one of the nickel coins I passed out two weeks ago? Step right up." But no one did.

He who makes light of the small loses the great.

This must have been the message Hill sought to convey to the hotel workers.

# 65

## All Boats Travel to Gain
## Honor or Profit

Once there was a palace on a mountaintop overlooking China's great river, the Yangtze. From the palace hundreds of boats could be seen plying the river each day.

One day, the emperor idly asked his chancellor, "How many boats do you think travel this river in a day?"

The chancellor's reply was instant. "Two, Your Majesty."

"Ridiculous. Are you blind? I can see several dozen right now. What do you mean by saying there are only two?"

"Sire, there appear to be many boats, but all of them are traveling to gain either honor or profit. That's why I say there are only two boats on the river: Honor and Profit."

The emperor was deeply impressed by the chancellor's apt answer.

Society grows increasingly competitive, fueled by people's strong desire to get ahead, stay on top, and soak up the limelight. Out of such motives—the desire for honor—people do reprehensible things like falsifying archaeological finds. Women who stake all on youth and beauty invest huge sums of money on cosmetic surgery, enduring great pain and risk. The reason men and women spend their waking hours worried about what other people think, with never a moment's peace, is because they are tormented by the desire for honor.

The desire for money is no less powerful. Here are two stories that illustrate the hold that greed has on people.

One hot summer day, an old man went to retrieve a watermelon cooling in the well, lost his balance, and fell in. His shocked wife hired a young man from the neighborhood to come and rescue him. When she told him what she had done, the old man shouted up from the bottom of the well, clutching his watermelon: "How much are you payin' him? Get him to lower his price!"

Another man devoted himself to piling up money. Money was his life. Since he couldn't see his money if he put it in the bank, he always kept it in a dresser drawer at home. He lived for the times when he came back after a hard day's work, went upstairs, and spread hundred-dollar bills over the floor just to gaze upon them. His savings steadily grew, and one day as he was spreading the money out as usual he unwittingly came too near the staircase, tumbled down, and died instantly from a broken neck. Clenched tightly in his fist was a wad of bills. Strange as it may seem, this is a true story.

People rejoice when they resolve a difficult problem, get upset when they fail, are delighted with the purchase of their first home, weep when their possessions go up in smoke, congratulate themselves on achieving fame, are downcast when vilified, get excited over a sudden windfall, fume and blame others when they lose money. Everyone chases honor and fame, everyone struggles to gain wealth and possessions.

The chancellor was right. There is nothing but Honor and Profit.

# 66

## To Cause Great Damage for a Slight Gain Is the Way of a Fool

Monkey, the hero of the Chinese classic *Journey to the West*, was a trickster who enjoyed superpowers. One day he challenged the Buddha to a contest to see whose powers were greater.

When Buddha accepted, Monkey quickly summoned a magical cloud that whisked him off at top speed. He returned after flying a vast distance and said with a swagger, "There! See what I can do?"

"Is that your best effort?"

"No one could do more."

"While you were flying, did you see five great mountains?"

"I did."

"What did you write on the top of the one in the middle?"

"I wrote 'Monkey has conquered this mountain'—but how did you know?"

As Monkey gaped in amazement, the Buddha displayed his hand and said, "See, you wrote the words on the tip of my middle finger."

As this episode shows, Monkey was gifted yet vain, and not half as clever as he thought he was. Monkeys are said to be the next highest animals after humans; just how clever are they? The following episodes give some idea.

Five scientists researching simian intelligence approached a mountain cave where a band of monkeys lived and fired blanks to chase them out. The surprised monkeys dashed out of the cave and up a nearby tree, where they clung as they stared down suspiciously at the humans. Under the monkeys' watchful eyes, the researchers all went into the cave, then one by one slowly walked out and scattered.

What happened next was interesting. After just three people had emerged, the monkeys descended the tree and went back to their cave, apparently under the impression that the coast was clear. On seeing the others they were thunderstruck, and fled back to the safety of the treetop.

The researchers repeated the experiment, and established conclusively that the monkeys could count to three.

At night, these same monkeys would go out in a band to steal radishes and burdock from nearby fields. When they pulled up one vegetable, they would hold it carefully in their arms, but every time they pulled up another one, they would drop the one they already had. When, after working steadily all night, they went home at dawn, each monkey would be carrying under its arm only one vegetable—the last one it had pulled up. For all the damage they did to the fields, the benefit they gained was minimal.

To cause great damage for a slight gain is the way of a fool.

National and tribal leaders around the world who, lacking perspective, respond to violence with violence, show no more wisdom than a pack of monkeys.

# 67

## People Who Reduce Everything to Logic Are Not Loved

Once there was a man who loathed anything that smacked of religion. "I can't stand the sight of a priest," he used to declare. "When I die, don't do anything stupid like hold a funeral. Just cremate my remains and scatter them from on high. Or if that's too much trouble, throw them in the river."

But life is uncertain. Sadly, the man's only son met with an untimely death. The grief-stricken father bathed and dressed his son's body and then went to one of his detested temples. He bowed to the head priest and said, "Please put on a fine funeral for the repose of my beloved boy's soul."

After the funeral, the boy's ashes were laid in the temple cemetery.

It snowed that day. The man went up to his son's grave and tenderly brushed away the snow with his hand, then laid down some oranges and sweets he had brought. Placing his palms together, he said, "Son, you must be cold. Here, I brought you these. Eat up." He sounded exactly as if he were speaking to someone who was very much alive. He lingered by the grave for a long time, people said.

Surely the man had not suddenly acquired a belief in the afterlife, yet something compelled him to behave as he did. Crushed with grief, he felt driven to arrange for a fine funeral and visit the grave.

In fact, self-styled atheists frequently call on pastors or priests to perform wedding ceremonies or conduct funerals. They can't help themselves. In Japan, ancient Shinto prayers are recited at the launching of a nuclear-powered ship. To a disinterested observer all this might seem strange, but there is something undeniably instinctive in the emotions.

Reducing everything to sheer logic always alienates others, because it ignores this deep-seated human trait. How much we miss out on in life as a result!

# 68

## Winning the Lottery Will Happen to Me, Disaster to Somebody Else

Long ago, a husband and wife who ran an inn heard that Japanese ginger could cause forgetfulness. One day a man who looked wealthy, carrying a great big bag, came and booked a room. Hoping to make him forget his bag when he left, the greedy couple decided to offer him a meal consisting entirely of ginger: ginger soup, stewed ginger, ginger salad, and so on.

When she brought him his tray, the wife said apologetically, "We are country folk and haven't much to offer. I made a few dishes using ginger from our garden. Please help yourself."

The customer was overjoyed. "Ginger, is it! My favorite. Looks delicious!"

As they went to sleep, the couple whispered that if they

just served ginger again for breakfast, he would be sure to go off and leave his bag. "I'll buy you a fine dress," the husband promised, "and maybe get me some fancy clothes too." Dreaming of such things, they went to sleep.

In the morning, she took in the breakfast tray. "Good morning, sir. I'm sorry I can't you offer anything fancier, but you were so pleased with last night's supper that I took the liberty of cooking ginger again this morning."

"Excellent. I see! Ginger-flavored soup, stewed ginger, fried ginger. Yum, yum."

When he had finished his meal, the customer waved goodbye and set off in fine spirits.

"Well," said the husband, "I'll go right up and search his room! I'm sure he must have forgotten something. Let's see, maybe in the closet? Or the bookcase? I know, it must be in the bathroom. Hmm, nothing under the desk. I'll lift up the floorboards and check. Nothing there either. That's funny, he didn't forget anything after all!"

Just then the wife came running. "Oh no!" she said. "We forgot to have him pay his bill!"

A man and his wife were talking eagerly about what they would do when they won the lottery.

"What if we win a hundred million dollars?"

"Let's go pick it up together."

"Someone might try to rob us."

"We should take it straight to the bank."

"What do you want to spend it on?" asked the husband.

"A big house," answered the wife. "And a piano for our daughter."

"I think I'll get a fancy car."

"Good idea. We could all go on a trip somewhere far away."

Just then their daughter came in and burst out laughing. "What are you talking about! You'll never win the lottery. Talk about counting your chickens before they're hatched!"

Disasters will happen to other people; good things will happen to me. That's what we all assume.

# 69

# The World Doesn't Work the Way We Wish It Did

A mother summoned her daughter and said, "Dear, it's time you thought about marriage. We've had two offers for your hand."

The girl blushed.

"One of your suitors is quite wealthy, but not so very handsome. The other one is extremely handsome, but hasn't got any money. It's your life, so you should be the one to choose between them. Think it over and tell me your decision."

The mother handed her a pair of photographs. The girl looked shyly back and forth from one to the other, but didn't say a word.

"If it's hard for you to say, here's what I'll do. I'll turn my back, and while I'm not looking you bare one shoulder.

If you want to marry the rich man, make it the right shoulder, and if you want to marry the handsome man, make it the left shoulder." The mother turned around and waited.

"Are you ready? Let me see." When she turned back again, the daughter had bared both shoulders. "What's this?"

The daughter explained. "I want the rich man for my husband by day, and the handsome man for my husband by night."

Among Aesop's fables is the following story.

A middle-aged man was in love with two women. One of them was much younger than he, the other was several years his elder. So that he would look younger, every night after dinner the younger woman would pillow his head in her lap and pull out his gray hairs.

The older woman didn't like for him to look younger than her, so every morning after breakfast she carefully pulled out black hairs from his head. The result was that the man soon found himself entirely bald.

The moral of the story, writes Aesop, is "Yield to all and you will soon have nothing to yield."

Sometimes couples have wealth but no children. No matter how they struggle, they cannot conceive a child. Others have many children but no wealth to speak of, and no matter how hard they work they cannot save any money. Some people have attractive features but wish they were taller. Others have elegant physiques, tall and slim, but are unhappy with their eyes or nose.

No one can have it all.

# 70

## Like the Earth, Women Are Strong and Unmoving

A man who failed in business came home and told his wife despondently, "I'm finished. You might as well know the truth. Everything of ours is being repossessed, down to the last stick of furniture." He expected her to wail, but instead she smiled. "That's too bad," she said, "but tell me—are you being taken away too?"

"No, that won't happen," he said.

"What about me?"

"No, no, this has nothing to do with you."

"And our son?"

"They won't touch him."

"Then you're wrong, dear, we aren't losing everything. Our greatest treasures are safe—our health and our precious son, with his whole life ahead of him. We're just taking a little detour, that's all. If we put our minds to it, we can still get all the money and possessions we could possibly want."

Her encouragement raised the man's spirits immediately, and he was able to weather the crisis.

Scientists once did an experiment where they put rabbits' legs in casts. The bucks grew angry and did all they could to free themselves, shaking their heads and biting at the cast. They paid no attention to their feed and only gnawed away in futility. The does, however, only gnawed for the first hour or so. When they saw the task was hopeless, they gave up and proceeded to eat and sleep as needed without wearing themselves out. As might be expected, it was the bucks who were first to weaken and die.

The foolish weakness of the bucks and the innate strength of the does have their echo in the behavior of men and women.

Come to think of it, women generally have a longer lifespan than men. Like the earth itself, women are strong and unmoving.

# 71

## Perseverance Is Greater than Proficiency
### *Cūḍa-panthaka's Perseverance at Cleaning*

One of Śākyamuni's greatest disciples, Cūḍa-panthaka, was dull by birth and unable to remember even his own name. One day Śākyamuni found him crying and asked him kindly, "Why are you so sad?"

Weeping bitterly, Cūḍa-panthaka lamented, "Why was I born stupid?"

"Cheer up," said Śākyamuni. "You are aware of your foolishness, but there are many fools who think themselves wise. Being aware of one's stupidity is next to enlightenment." He handed Cūḍa-panthaka a broom and instructed him to say while he worked, "I sweep the dust away. I wash the dirt away."

Cūḍa-panthaka tried desperately to remember those sacred phrases from the Buddha, but whenever he remembered one, he forgot the other. Even so, he kept at this practice for twenty years.

Once during those twenty years, Śākyamuni complimented Cūḍa-panthaka on his constant diligent effort. "No matter how many years you keep sweeping, you grow no better at it, and yet that does not cause you to give up. As important as making progress is, persevering in the same endeavor is even more important. It is an admirable trait—one that I do not see in my other disciples."

In time Cūḍa-panthaka realized that dust and dirt did not only accumulate where he thought they would, but in places he least expected. Surprised, he thought, "I knew I was stupid, but there's no telling how much more of my stupidity exists in places I don't even notice."

In the end Cūḍa-panthaka attained the enlightenment of an arhat, a stage at which one is worthy of receiving respect and offerings. Besides encountering a great teacher and the true teachings, it was his long years of effort and perseverance that crowned him with success.

# 72

# A Grand Champion Leaves an Opponent an Opening

Once there was a very strong wrestler among a party of sumo wrestlers on tour in Kyushu. Everyone predicted that he would be invincible. One of his supporters gushed, "At this rate you'll be a grand champion in no time!"

The wrestler answered with quiet dignity, "Thank you for saying so, but I am not grand champion material. It's not so much that my wrestling leaves opponents no opening as that I can't afford to leave them any. That is a failing on my part. The sumo wrestling of grand champions has a certain free and easy quality to it. A grand champion always gives his opponent an opening of some kind. Since I lack that ability, I can never reach the top. I am still a beginner, I am embarrassed to say."

This is a great saying by a self-aware man of truly admirable character.

Conversation with a person who leaves you no opening is suffocating. It is impossible to feel relaxed and intimate with such a person.

Someone who seems to have imperfections or to be lacking in some way has the potential to attract people and be loved. Like the mole on a beautiful woman's cheek, imperfections have a strange way of burrowing into our affections and winning us over.

The medieval swordsman Miyamoto Musashi showed his ultimate mastery of the art of sword-fighting by always coming at his opponent with his guard down. Only those who know their opponent and know themselves have the mental composure to act that way. It is an indispensable attribute of the truly great.

# 73

# Look to the Essence, Not the Form

Back in the late nineteenth century, one of Japan's first elementary school was established in the city of Osaka. One day the teacher told his pupils about an incident in the life of the great Chinese historian and scholar Sima Guang (1019–86). One time, when he was seven, Sima Guang and his friends were climbing for fun on a large jar of water when one of the children slipped and fell inside. The other children all ran home to tell their parents. Only Sima Guang stayed his ground, reasoning, "He'll drown before anyone can get here to save him. No matter how valuable a jar is, a human life is worth more." He smashed the jar and saved his friend's life. The teacher concluded, "Sima Guang left his mark on history because when he was a boy he had the courage to smash that jar."

The children were so inspired by this story that they each went straight home and smashed every jar in the kitchen they could lay hands on.

"What do you think you're doing!" Taken to task for this behavior by shocked family members, the children all answered boldly, "Go ask any of the other kids. The teacher said that if you want to grow up to be great, you have to start by breaking jars when you're little."

One child broke a pickle jar, another a miso jar . . . all over town, valuable jars lay in shards. This misunderstanding led to an unusual development, as parents across town protested against sending their children to school.

One of Śākyamuni's main disciples, Śāriputra, was doing seated meditation in a peaceful and secluded mountain spot when Vimalakīrti, a sage whom he had always admired, happened along and asked him what he was doing. As the answer seemed obvious, Śāriputra was put out and answered, with irritation, "I'm meditating!" Perceiving Śāriputra's distraction, Vimalakīrti retorted, "You call that meditating? If by 'meditation' you mean only sitting without moving, you might just as well say the trees around you are meditating, too." In this way he pointed out that Śāriputra was following only the outward form of meditation, having lost its true spirit.

When we pursue the outward form while neglecting the inner essence, the result is always pitiful.

# 74

# Don't Be Swayed This Way and That by Critics

Once a father and son ran a farm with little or no success. They failed at everything they tried their hand at, and were forced to sell off their furniture and other possessions one by one to make ends meet. Finally all they had left was a small horse. After talking it over, they decided to take the horse to town to sell it, too.

Soon after they set off, they passed a man heading the other way and heard him murmur, "Two men walking a horse? That's strange. Why doesn't one of them ride?" The farmer thought this made sense, and had his son get up and ride. They continued on this way, the father leading the pony, until before long they came upon another traveler. This one said under his breath, "Look at that! The son takes it easy, making his poor old father do the work. For shame!"

Nodding agreement, the father turned to his son and said, "I'll ride now. You can lead the horse." And so they traded places.

The next one they passed muttered, "Look at that. The father rides in comfort and makes his son lead the horse. Some parents have no consideration."

The father saw the justice of this remark, and invited his son to climb up behind him. On they went, both of them riding the little horse.

The next one they encountered murmured indignantly, "What a sight! Two grown men on a pony! Where's their common sense?"

Father and son nodded to each other in agreement. Together they tied up the horse's legs, fastened them to a pole, and carried the animal into town on their shoulders. They walked hither and yon trying to sell it, but found no takers. In the end, as they were crossing a long bridge, a car came along and frightened the little horse so much that it fell into the river and drowned.

Though it's important to listen to opinions of others, if

you are constantly swayed by people's criticism, you'll never get the job done.

# 75

## A Mother's Tongue Can Determine the Course of Her Child's Life

Léon Gambetta, a poor grocer's son, grew up to become a great French statesman of the nineteenth century. This is the inspiring story of how his mother helped him realize his dream.

When Gambetta was around fifteen, he was sent off to be a tailor's apprentice but came back home after only a few months. His quick-tempered father gave him a tongue-lashing and ordered him to work in the family grocery store. His mother, seeing how depressed he was, took pity on him and quietly asked why he had quit the apprenticeship.

"It didn't suit me."

"Then what would suit you?"

"I want to be a great statesman and work for the common good."

"Great aspirations come to nothing if you give up along the way."

"I'll do it, no matter how much I suffer."

"How much money will you need?"

"If I had three hundred francs, I could go to Paris and find a job. I swear I can make my dream come true."

"If you're that determined, I'll find a way to raise the money."

Soon the determined mother laid before her son the money she had raised. "Here!" she told him. "Take this and use it to accomplish your goal."

Gambetta was amazed. "We are poor. Where did all this money come from?"

"I borrowed it."

"Nobody would lend such a large sum of money without collateral."

"Of course I put up collateral."

"What do we have that's worth this much? Nothing!"

"Not at all. I used my tongue as collateral. I told him you were going to become a great statesman and had to have this money to do it. I promised him you would accomplish your goal and assured him I would pay back every penny when you did." Gambetta vowed, "I will not make a liar of my mother!"

His strenuous efforts paid off, and in the end he did become a prominent statesman.

A mother's tongue can determine the course of her child's life. And through her children a mother can change the world.

# 76

## The Resolve of a Beautiful Woman

When he was a hot-blooded youth of eighteen, the samurai Endo Morito became fascinated with a woman of remarkable beauty. He tracked down her identity and found to his dismay that she was Kesa, the wife of Minamoto Wataru, his relative and a palace guard. He was distressed to learn this, but his love only grew stronger. Finally, unable to contain himself, he went to the girl's mother and begged her to let him have Kesa, adding, "I fully realize the impossibility of this request, but if it is not granted, I will have no choice but to kill all who stand in my way."

Not knowing what to do at this reckless declaration of love, Kesa's mother summoned her daughter and told her everything. Kesa was shocked and saddened, but at last she came to a decision. "Mother, don't worry. It's too bad for my husband, but I choose Morito."

Soon after that she went to see Morito to tell him her decision, but she appeared downcast.

"Is something wrong, dearest?" he asked.

"I am happy to be loved by you, but the thought of my husband tortures me. If only he weren't alive . . ."

"I understand. Let me take care of it."

"Nothing could make me happier."

After coming to this understanding with Kesa, Morito sneaked into Wataru's bedroom one night and beheaded him as he lay sleeping. Exulting that at last the beautiful Kesa was his alone, he held up the severed head in the moonlight—only to see that it was the head of the woman he loved more than life itself.

He went into despair, threw himself on the ground in an agony of regret, and in the end took renounced the world and became a monk. The eminent monk Mongaku was none other than he.

After Kesa's death, in her letterbox they found a note declaring her real love for her husband. The beauty of the century protected her virtue with her life and prevented two men from stumbling into great darkness.

# 77

## "This Painting Is a Fake"
### *The Significance of Actual Experience*

People flocked to see a certain painter's exhibition. There was always an especially large crowd in front of his most famous painting, a depiction of a mother feeding her child. Concerned about what people might be saying about his work, the painter mingled with them anonymously and listened.

"This is his best work, isn't it." Everyone paused in front of that same painting, the one he was proudest of, and praised it to the skies. The painter was secretly feeling smug, when he happened to see a woman murmur, "This painting is a fake," and walk away. He felt a cold shock. Whether it was the incisive comment of an eminent critic or the off-the-cuff remark of a rank amateur, he didn't know, but he couldn't let it pass. He followed after the woman and quietly introduced himself.

"I am the painter of that work. May I ask why you called it a fake?"

The woman looked rather embarrassed, but she explained, "When a woman feeds a child, she always opens her own mouth first. The mouth of the woman in that painting is closed. That's why I said it is a fake. Please forgive me."

Impressed by the importance of actual experience, the painter thanked her sincerely and redid the painting.

The third Tokugawa shogun, Iemitsu, once asked his retainers this question: "When do you feel most at ease?"

One man said, "I never feel so at ease as when, after waiting to relieve myself, I can comfortably move my bowels."

Iemitsu was enraged. "What insolence! How dare you say such a thing!" He sentenced the man to detention.

Some days later when Iemitsu was out falcon hunting, he felt an attack of diarrhea coming on—but there was no toilet around. For the master of the realm to empty his bowels on the ground in front of everyone was unthinkable, so he waited while his men hurriedly fashioned a toilet.

"Isn't it ready yet?" he chafed. He felt ready to explode.

"Almost, sire."

When at length Iemitsu dashed to the makeshift toilet, he remembered the retainer he had sentenced to detention. He ordered him released and given a raise in stipend.

# 78

## "No One in This World Seeks to Do Good More than I Myself," Said the Buddha

Shockingly, the Buddha's disciple Aniruddha nodded off one day in the middle of a sermon. When the sermon was over, Śākyamuni summoned him and asked quietly, "What is your purpose in seeking the way of Buddhism?"

"It is to resolve the crucial matter of birth-and-death," answered Aniruddha without hesitation.

"Though you were brought up in a wealthy home, you are firm in purpose. Why then did you nod off?"

Deeply moved by the Buddha's compassionate reproach, Aniruddha begged his forgiveness and swore never to sleep again as long as he lived. Sure enough, from that day on he devoted himself to ascetic practice without sleeping. When prolonged lack of sleep began to affect his eyesight, Śākyamuni told him, "You must be like the string of a lyre, that is taut when it should be taut and loose when it should be loose. Excessive effort leads to regret, while laziness gives rise to blind passions. It is best to take the middle way."

Although told by a doctor that sleep would cure his eyesight, Aniruddha continued to observe his vow with firm determination, until in the end he went stone blind. This was truly a selfless act undertaken at the risk of his very life. In the process, he gained a profound inner eye and went on to become one of the Buddha's top ten disciples.

The day after he lost his eyesight, Aniruddha was trying unsuccessfully to thread a needle to mend his worn-out robe. He called out, "Would someone seeking to do good please thread this needle for me?"

A voice replied, "I would like very much to do it." It was none other than Śākyamuni Buddha himself.

Amazed, Aniruddha replied in awe, "But you have achieved all goodness and virtue!"

The Buddha answered, "Even though one has attained the enlightenment of a buddha, that is no reason to neglect small acts of good. No one in this world seeks to do good more than I myself."

# 79

# What Makes a Master Swordsmith

This happened in fourteenth-century Japan. In a bid to decide who was the greatest swordsmith in the land, eighteen people were chosen, and each one made a sword. Among the submissions were swords by master smiths Okazaki Masamune and Go Yoshihiro. After rigorous examination, Masamune's sword was judged the best.

Yoshihiro was from central Honshu, near the Japan Sea, and enjoyed a reputation as the finest swordsmith of the day. He was full of braggadocio and unable to forgive anyone who got the better of him. "There must be some explanation," he thought, deeply disgruntled. "Masamune must have bribed the judges."

He traveled east to see his rival in Kamakura, determined to settle the matter with a duel. When he arrived,

Masamune was just tempering a blade. Sounds of rhythmic hammering came from within the foundry. Yoshihiro cautiously looked inside and was astonished by what he saw.

Inside the spotless foundry, Masamune was dressed in formal *hakama* and wielded the hammer with clean, regular motions. There was something majestic in his appearance.

Suspecting nothing, Masamune welcomed his visitor from afar with full hospitality.

Yoshihiro made a full confession. "Until now I doubted you, resented you, and was even determined to challenge you to a duel, but that was a grave mistake. Now I have seen the dignity with which you work, pouring yourself heart and soul into the making of a sword. In comparison, when I get hot I strip down, and when I'm thirsty I drink my fill. In fact there is no comparison between us. You have shown me that technical skill and strength alone are not enough to make someone a true master."

Yoshihiro then begged Masamune to take him on as his disciple. At first Masamune modestly declined, but Yoshihiro insisted, and so in the end he agreed.

# 80

## Why So Few Succeed

Ninomiya Sontoku, the nineteenth-century Japanese agriculturist, was seated at dinner with his family. He reached out to help himself to some pickled radish, and found that several of the slices were connected, as the knife had failed to cut all the way through. Indicating the poorly cut slices, Sontoku commented, "This shows the importance of following through in all you do. Serving pickled radish is by no means easy. You have to lift off the heavy stone on the jar, remove the lid, and pull out a radish covered in rice bran. Then, after replacing the lid and the stone, you have to wash off the radish, slice it up, and arrange the slices on a serving dish. But if you fail to use enough strength when slicing it, you end up with something like this, which would be rude to serve company.

"Most people can do eighty or ninety percent of a task, but they fail to do that last ten percent carefully. That's what makes the difference between success and failure. Remember, it's always the last bit that makes the difference."

The author and educator Sugi Toshisuke was once the head of First High School, today's the University of Tokyo. He used to relate how, after graduating from college, he paid a call at the home of statesman Shinagawa Yajiro, a fellow native of Yamaguchi Prefecture whose life had often been in peril at the tumultuous time of the Meiji Restoration. It was an age when college graduates were rare, and highly revered in society.

As Sugi came strutting proudly up the walk, Shinagawa, seated on his veranda, told him, "Just remember, graduation for a human being is a funeral. If you don't keep that in mind you won't carry anything through in life." The phrase "graduation for a human being" became Sugi's lifelong motto.

The world of professional sumo wrestling is rigidly hierarchical. It is said that depending on your placement in the rankings, you may be treated like a lord, a servant, or a worm. This uncompromising attitude is part of what makes sumo sumo. One third of all newcomers quit within the first year. Most of the rest quit in four or five years, unable to attain the rank of junior-grade wrestler. One in twenty of the junior-grade wrestlers makes it on to the senior-grade division, and barely one in 150 becomes a champion.

How hard it is to carry through to the end without any letup in focus, maintaining one's original determination all the way. Small wonder that so few succeed.

# 81

## "Someone Came Asking for Money, But He Didn't Rob Me"

Shichiri Gojun, the head of a temple in Kyushu, was one of the greatest priests of modern times. One night a thief burst into the room where he was sleeping and brandished a short sword. The thief grew uncomfortable as Shichiri looked him full in the face. "Your money or your life. Be quick about it!"

"The money is in the decorative box at the back of the alcove," said Shichiri calmly. As the thief scooped up the box and started to dash off, he added, "Wait just a moment."

"What is it?" the thief said, glaring.

Shichiri spoke calmly. "That money is here on trust from Buddha. Go to the main hall and thank him before you go." He said this with a virtue and authority that must have been highly impressive, for the thief headed straight to the main hall and bowed his head in gratitude before taking off.

Soon a summons came from the police, who informed Shichiri that the thief had been captured. The saintly priest then had this appealing conversation with a stern officer:

"When someone steals your money or valuables, you must file a report right away."

"But I wasn't robbed, officer, I'm sure of it."

"Say what you will, the thief has already confessed."

"There must be some mistake. It's true that a man came by one night wanting money. I gave him some and told him to thank Buddha for it. I wasn't robbed."

Eventually, on hearing that the man had served his time and was going to be released from prison, the priest decided to take him in. "He and I have a connection from another life. I need an accountant in the temple, so it's perfect. He can come work for me."

The man was so moved that he made a fresh start in life and never lost his way again.

Of the untold billions of people living on this planet, those who become parent and child, siblings, husband and wife, or friends must share especially strong bonds from earlier lives. Passengers on a ship gather from near and far to make the journey together, only to scatter again once they arrive on shore. A flock of birds spends the night perched together in a single tree, but at the break of dawn each one flies off alone in search of food.

Our association in this life is only for a night, until we reach the far shore.

When we realize this, every fellow traveler, no matter how disagreeable, becomes someone with whom we feel a deep connection.

# 82

## "Head into the Wind!"

*Facing Life's Storms*

Once a monstrous typhoon made a direct hit on Japan. Inside a country school, pupils and teacher sat in mortal terror as the building swayed and creaked. No one knew what to do.

Finally the teacher jumped up. "Everyone, go out and face the wind!" The children obediently ran outside—only to be blown about at the mercy of the wind. Instinctively, they tried to walk downwind.

"No!" shouted the teacher. "Crawl into the paddy, hold tight to the rice stalks, and head INTO the wind!"

Surprised at the ferocity in the teacher's voice, the children did as they were told. Soon the school building downwind from them collapsed with a great crash, but luckily no one was killed or injured.

Life is like that. We know it's important to face trials head-on with calm and courage, but doing so is hard.

Even little things can be grating. From the time we get up till the time we go to bed, one thing after another gets under our skin. The tap water may be too cold or too hot, the coffee too strong or too weak. Weather is seldom just to our liking, and people at home and at work can be impossible to get along with. On top of it all, disasters and tragedies befall us. Life brings suffering, sadness, and pain. Happiness is rare.

The way to deal with life's frustrations is to face them individually, head-on, in the moment. "Get through this somehow." When you face a trial, tell yourself, "Just get through it," and the burden will ease. When you are suffering, and showing kindness to others seems impossible, tell yourself, "Just get through this," and you can do it with a smile. When courage is needed, tell yourself, "Just get through it," and find strength to forgive. Walk forward step by step into the storms of suffering, telling yourself, "Just get through this!"

# AFTERWORD

Japanese newspapers often contain full-page advertisements for fortune-telling based on one's carved personal seal. When I think how much such advertising must cost, my mind reels. Even so, those who advertise turn a profit, which just goes to show you how many people believe fortune-tellers can tell them whether their luck is good or bad—whether their future holds calamity or blessing.

In fact there are all sorts of fortune-tellers. Some read your palm, others read the aspect of your house or family grave, still others tell you what your lucky and unlucky days are. All stay in business for one reason: people believe that fortune-telling has some connection to their happiness or unhappiness in this world. This belief is deep-rooted, but Buddhism treats all forms of divination, without exception, as sheer superstition.

True happiness comes not from the shape of your seal or the lines of your palm, Buddhism tells us, but from doing good deeds in your daily life. Good deeds yield good results; bad deeds yield bad results; my deeds yield my results. No pumpkin seed ever produced an eggplant. Only seeds that are planted bring results.

Sometimes results appear right away, but other times the waiting time may be decades or may even extend into the next lifetime. Whether the process is quick or slow, in the end every deed bears fruits. The law of cause and effect operates completely independently of our wishes and convenience. To live each day with diligence, believing in this great law, is the way of the Buddhist, the way of the Shinran follower.

Some of the traits most lacking in people today are diligence and effort. People choose the easy path, just as water flows downhill. They want results without effort, like those who dream of winning big in the lottery.

Dogs wag their tails at those who feed them, howl and snap at those who don't. Human nature isn't much different. We have become rather like beasts—perhaps because society puts so much emphasis on schools and intellectual education while ignoring the importance of moral education.

A woman once asked an eminent priest about educating her baby and was told, "It's too late."

"But he's still a newborn," she protested.

"To educate him properly," said the priest, "I needed to start with *your* mother."

The woman was amazed.

> Time and again,
> someone took time and effort:
> chrysanthemum bloom.

Even producing a beautiful, fragrant flower cannot be done overnight. Raising a child to become a person of integrity is no easy task. Proper schooling is of course important, but what they absorb from parents, and particularly from parents' unspoken attitudes, is far more important in building character. How a child turns out depends on its parents' actions.

There is an old English saying: "The hand that rocks the cradle is the hand that rules the world."

If parenthood consists merely in giving birth, then we are no different from animals. Those who live in ignorance of the law of cause and effect, living lives of self-indulgence and vice, will surely suffer in this world: their hearts filled with enmity, they will curse their miserable lives. They bring ruin on themselves and plunge their children into adversity as well. If the needle does not go in a straight line, the stitches will not lie straight. Parents must teach by example.

"You aren't qualified to be a parent unless you know at least a hundred fairy tales and edifying stories," declares one educator. Interesting stories can fill small souls with determination, nurturing an invincible spirit and ridding the mind of indolence, polishing it to diamond brightness.

Those who walk toward the light inevitably prosper; those who run into the darkness inevitably come to ruin. I have endeavored to press on, step by step, into the light, accompanied by others who share ties with Buddhism. It would make me very happy if the stories here prove useful to readers.

Kentetsu Takamori

The afterword is a translation of the introduction to *Hikari ni mukatte hyaku no hanataba* by Kentetsu Takamori.

KENTETSU TAKAMORI has dedicated his life to faithfully conveying the teachings of Shinran (1173–1263), the founder of the True Pure Land School. He has lectured throughout Japan and worldwide on Buddhism for more than half a century. He is the author of several best-selling titles in Japanese and the chair of the Buddhist organization Jodo Shinshu Shinrankai.

His other works available in English are *You Were Born for a Reason: The Real Purpose of Life* (2001), *Something You Forgot . . . Along the Way: Stories of Wisdom and Learning* (2009), and *Unlocking Tannisho: Shinran's Words on the Pure Land Path* (2011).

He lives with his wife and their dog in a small town in Toyama Prefecture overlooking the Japan Sea.

## To the Reader

Please take a minute to share your thoughts with us.
We want to know how the stories in this book affected you.
Which were your favorites, and why?
Your comments will be helpful in planning future titles.
Please email us at info@i-ipi.com

Or write us at Ichimannendo Publishing, Inc. (IPI),
970 West 190th Street, Suite 920, Torrance, CA 90502

For more information on this and other books by
Ichimannendo Publishing, Inc., please visit our website at
www.i-ipi.com

# Ichimannendo Publishing, Inc.

## Something You Forgot ... Along the Way
### *Stories of Wisdom and Learning*

By Kentetsu Takamori

This book introduces sixty-five heart-warming stories that show what it means to learn from life's events. These simple yet beautiful tales invite us to look deeper into almost any situation in life. In the tradition of Aesop's Fables each story concludes with a moral lesson.

This book was originally published in Japanese by Ichimannendo Publishing Co. Ltd. It is part of a Japanese series which has sold over a million copies.

List Price: US$11.95
192 pages/Paperback/
7.4×5.1 inches
ISBN978-0-9790471-1-4

## YOU WERE BORN FOR A REASON
### *The Real Purpose of Life*

By Kentetsu Takamori,
Daiji Akehashi, and Kentaro Ito

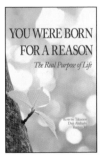

What is the meaning of life? Where can we find true happiness that will never fade away? This book addresses these all-important questions head-on.

*YOU WERE BORN FOR A REASON* is the English translation of the runaway best-selling book on Buddhism, *Naze ikiru,* which has sold 700,000 copies since its publication in Japanese in 2001 and is still going strong.

List Price: US$16.95
236 pages/Hardcover/
9.3×6.3 inches
ISBN978-0-9790471-0-7